Thanks to Quirk Books for the opportunity to do this project. Special thanks to Mary Ellen Wilson and Jenny Kraemer for helping to make it extra special. And thank you to the homemakers who provided all the useful information featured in this book.

Library of Congress Cataloging in Publication Number: 2010924451

ISBN: 978-1-59474-461-7

Printed in China

Typeset in Neutraface and Century Old Style

Art direction by Jenny Kraemer
Production management by Melissa Jacobson

Distributed in North America by Chronicle Books
680 Second Street
San Francisco, CA 94107

10 9 8 7 6 5 4 3 2 1

Quirk Books
215 Church Street
Philadelphia, PA 19106
www.irreference.com
www.quirkbooks.com

HOME ECONOMICS

VINTAGE ADVICE and PRACTICAL SCIENCE for the 21st-CENTURY HOUSEHOLD

compiled by
JENNIFER McKNIGHT TRONTZ

QUIRK BOOKS
PHILADELPHIA

CONTENTS

INTRODUCTION

Technology has made life easier for billions of people, but one of its greatest benefits is its contribution to women's rights. Liberated from the need to have someone at home all day long, women could work in offices, flip burgers, run banks. Home economics ("home ec" to dwindling generations of high school students) was seen as a lowering of horizons, regressive even.

Home Economics: Vintage Advice and Practical Science for the 21st-Century Household revisits the discipline's textbooks and lessons dating from the 1900s to the 1940s, when homemaking was considered a profession unto itself, and a noble (if unpaid) one at that. It is not necessarily a call for a return to simpler times, but a celebration of the vast amount of critical knowledge once entrusted to the nation's homemakers and now in need of a good dose of dusting.

Even a cursory review of the lessons gives a sense of how much know-how has been lost: how to hand wash different fabrics; which substances remove which stains; troubleshooting the many types of tragedy known as "cake failure." Some lessons are quaint; others are wishful. Many are picky. But even the most basic of lessons are, seen from the distance of our times, almost clever in their simplicity. Sure, you know how to use a broom. But do you sweep in small strokes, away from you so as not to snare dust in your clothing? Do you know which colors clash? Did you ever consider that dining room curtains should be easily washable, to get rid of food odors?

Most home economics texts stressed the *science* of homemaking, and they were not being cute. The homemaker had to know what vitamins and nutrients each member of her family needed, and which foods provided them for the least money. She learned that the tough cut of meat was as nutritious as the filet—and through scientific knowledge, she could make it just as tasty.

Some practices that pass for retro chic today were considered sound living. No one thought it radical to use natural cleaners like baking soda and vinegar. A jacket with a worn elbow was not tossed, but patched. Hose and socks were darned, not ditched. There were guidelines for using vegetables to compensate for a "growing distaste for animal food," but there were also tips that carnivores could take to heart, such as saving bacon grease to use in the crust of meat pies.

Some lessons would be considered biting commentary today. "Imitations of choice woods may serve one's needs," one book professed, "but it is not thrifty to pay choice-wood prices for imitations." What would gourmet groceries make of the dictum that there is "no connection between nutritive value and the price of food"? And what is the admonition that "paying more than one can afford is one of the weaknesses of installment buying" if not a missile strike against modern capitalism?

These lessons were the compilation of centuries of trial and error, boom and bust, sickness and health, and formed the connective tissue between the family and society. The home was an institution, to be economically managed so that the best and most efficient citizens would be given to the community. The plainly titled 1913 textbook *Shelter and Clothing* let it be known exactly what was at stake: "Upon the privacy and sanctity of the home rests the strength of democracy."

The laboratory for the home-making studies.

"Housekeeping is becoming more and more a matter of science, and the laurels are bound to fall to the woman who conducts her household in a business-like way."

Successful Economical Living

The true economy of housekeeping is simply the art of gathering up all the fragments so that nothing is lost. This applies to fragments of both *materials* and *time*. (After all, *time* is *money*.) Nothing should be thrown away so long as it is possible to make any use of it, however trifling that use may be. And whatever be the size of the family, every member should be employed either in earning or saving money. The care of the home and the management of all household duties are in the homemaker's hands. A house becomes a home when it is made a happy, healthful, restful, and attractive place in which to live. Isn't that what we all wish for?

Home economics teaches how to manage a house in such a way that money and income are wisely spent. It means learning to do the household work systematically and well. It means learning to entertain one's friends in a simple yet hospitable way, and to make home the happiest kind of place. Because, after all, the home is really the center of things.

DOMESTIC MANAGEMENT
AND SYSTEMS

Housekeeping of today takes its place among the professions. The modern woman plans, directs, and guides the work of the home. She grasps the responsibilities of her position, puts forth all her energy and ability in directing the home life as a business. Housekeeping is becoming more and more a matter of science, and the laurels are bound to fall to the woman who conducts her household in a business-like way.

Good home management includes the selection and care of all materials used in the home and the keeping of accurate household accounts. If one is ignorant of the right kind of food to eat, of the proper clothing to wear, of the best kind of sanitary conditions of one's house, of the laws of health, of simple pleasures and the ways of right living, how can one spend wisely the necessary money for these things in order to make the home a happy, healthful place? One of the most important features of good home management is a *system*. Another is a *budget*.

SETTING UP A SYSTEM, OR ROUTINE. A good habit to form is regularity of living. Do you not feel better when you get up at the right time, start work promptly, and do your other duties on time? People like structure, and having a system helps. With a system, each day and week has its special duties to be performed, and each member of the household knows what he or she is responsible for. Here is a sample routine for a productive week of housework:

Mondays	Baking and meal preparation
Tuesdays	Washing, ironing, mending
Wednesdays	Cleaning of 8 windows, at 10 minutes each
Thursdays	Kitchen-shelf or pantry cleaning
Fridays	Alternate silver or furniture polishing

THE BENEFITS OF A BUDGET. Wise spending is more important than the most diligent saving, hence, the need for a *budget*—a plan for spending money. A budget always precedes the spending of money and may be made for a month, a half year, or a year in advance. The family must know how to spend its income to enable each member to attain a maximum of health, comfort, recreation, and financial protection without needless effort and worry.

Careful planning of the family expenditures means a successful use of the family *income*, or all the money that comes into the home from various sources. The chief source is generally salary or wages, or profits made in a business or in operating a farm. Another important source is the work that the homemaker does in the home. If she did not do the work of managing and keeping the home and caring for the children, someone else would have to be paid for this. The responsibility for spending the income belongs to each member of the family. All members must be willing to do their share in making the budget and following it in order that the whole family may receive the most benefits by living within its income.

SHARING IN THE ECONOMICS OF THE FAMILY. It is a wise plan for a family to devote one evening a month to adding bills, paying bills, and determining whether they are living within their budget. It will help every member to be more careful in spending money. A child should be given an allowance each week. Even a very little tot can learn to spend her allowance without being too wasteful. To be economically independent gives every member of the family a feeling of self-respect and importance in the family and in the community.

Watch the little items, for they run up expenses in an astonishing way. Small wastes make big inroads into expenses and distinguish the skillful, thrifty housekeeper from the careless and inefficient one.

HOME BUDGET SYSTEM. In making a family budget, the first provisions should be made for food, shelter, clothing, and operating expenses. A good plan is to divide the yearly income according to months and weeks and to keep all expenses well within the limits. Set aside a percentage of the salary for each class of expenditures: shelter, clothing, food, etc. The chart below shows a sample budget breakdown; the amounts or percentages of the income that each family spends for these six groups of household expenses differ. As the income increases, the percentages of expenditures for some of the items usually increase in proportion, up to a certain point.

The following percentages are merely suggestions:
- Housing, 20% to 25% rent or (if a home is owned) mortgage, taxes, insurance, interest on mortgage, repairs (including painting).
- Food, 20% to 25% groceries and meals purchased outside the home.
- Clothing, 15% clothes, material for clothes, shoes, and accessories.
- Operating Expenses, 15% to 20% *a*. Family: light, fuel, telephone, water, laundry work, cleaning house or yard work, *b*. Personal: carfare, manicures, toilet articles, etc. *c*. Automobiles: gas, oil, repairs, insurance.

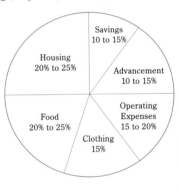

- Advancement (or development), 10% to 15% *a*. Education: school fees, tuition, books, magazines, lectures, etc. *b*. Health: medical and dental fees, drugs, glasses. *c*. Recreation: entertainments, vacations, etc. *d*. Benevolence: contributions to charity.
- Savings, 10% to 15% money, life insurance.

METHODS OF ORDERLY HOUSEHOLD ACCOUNTS. When the division of the family income has been decided upon, a system of bookkeeping will greatly aid in keeping track of each expenditure so that you know you are living within the stated amounts. This system of accounts should be simple and easy to keep. Receipts should be kept together and used to check up with the monthly statement. In case of error, these are of great value in correcting the account.

In keeping accounts, some method showing income and expenditures must be used so that a balance can easily be taken. The simplest form is to rule a blank book and enter the totals for each month. Rule your book like Table 1 below. Do the same for your income—with entries for earnings, gifts, allowance, and the like—and then reconcile your books each month.

Table 1. A Sample Budget

	JAN	FEB	MAR	APR	MAY	JUNE	JULY	AUG	SEP	OCT	NOV	DEC
Rent	...	....	....	.....	....	.....	....	.....	....	....	....	....
Fuel	...	....	....	.....	....	.....	....	.....	....	....	....	....
Light	...	....	....	.....	....	.....	....	.....	....	....	....	....
Grocer	...	....	....	.....	....	.....	....	.....	....	....	....	....
Dairy	...	....	....	.....	....	.....	....	.....	....	....	....	....
Clothing	...	....	....	.....	....	.....	....	.....	....	....	....	....
Operating expense	...	....	....	.....	....	.....	....	.....	....	....	....	....
Service	...	....	....	.....	....	.....	....	.....	....	....	....	....
Higher life	...	....	....	.....	....	.....	....	.....	....	....	....	....

BE A WISE CONSUMER

As the saying goes: Buyer beware. When the homemaker goes shopping, she has a responsibility of getting good value for her money. One of the first requisites of good buying is the ability to know standard qualities. By so doing, you will not be at the mercy of the salespeople. Another necessary thing is to know what you yourself need, so that a cleverly worded advertisement will not lure you into making unnecessary purchases. Keep a list of needed articles, and do your shopping accordingly. Caution: Always keep within your budget system.

WATCH FOR DECEPTIVE ADVERTISING. In order to be a wise buyer, it is necessary to be familiar with descriptive words used by manufacturers and merchants. One who shops for clothes, food, and household furnishings should know not only the quality and standards of goods and equipment but also the terms describing quality or grade. She should be on the alert to learn more about buying. If you have doubts about a product's worth or quality, walk away.

You should notice whether an advertisement:
- Advertises the quality of a product or appeals to a buyer's desire for beauty, romance, pride, or to a sense of fear. (The focus should be on quality.)
- Makes false or extravagant claims about products.
- Is sufficiently definite to give a clear idea about the quality and durability of goods.

THE DANGER OF CREDIT AND "EASY" PAYMENTS. Paying more than you can afford is one of the weaknesses of installment buying. Because payments are spread over a long period, they sound "easy" to some persons. Nothing should be bought on an installment plan without reasonable assurance that the purchaser will be able to meet all payments.

Perhaps the greatest drawback to installment buying is the carelessness with which people enter into buying contracts in not figuring how much interest-deferred payments will cost. Because the payment for goods is spread over a period of time, interest is charged to the buyer. Be sure you understand the credit terms (read the fine print!) and, most important, *do the math*.

SELECTING ITEMS FOR YOURSELF AND YOUR HOME. Never before in history has it been necessary for women to know so much about materials in order to select the necessities of life, to provide herself and her family with appropriate food, shelter, and clothing. This is woman's time to show her ingenuity in thrift and in the preservation of the essentials of life.

In buying, do not go to any except known firms that have established a reputation for reliability. If you're too busy to attend in person to your shopping, telephone calls certainly aid in making purchases. Mail-order houses are sometimes a help to the shopper, although because of community welfare, it is better to patronize local stores. Do not confine your buying entirely to telephoning, for nothing can equal personal visits. And it goes without saying to watch the sales. Much can be saved in buying out of season—many times a winter garment bought in December can be had at less than half the price the next January or March. Practice patience and your budget will thank you.

 A good shopper thinks out her needs most carefully and knows just how much money she has to spend. All of this careful planning saves one much time and money.

YOUR BODY, YOUR HOUSE

Do you know that your body, the real house in which you live, must be made attractive, must be kept clean, and its management must be planned? Indeed, one is a slacker if she is not well in these times.

Try your best to do the following:

✓ Sleep at least eight hours at night.
✓ Eat regularly, nourishing food; avoid overeating.
✓ Eat and drink slowly, and chew solid foods thoroughly.
✓ Avoid excess of eggs, meat, salt, sweets, and seasoned foods.
✓ Drink plenty of water; not too much tea and coffee.
✓ Exercise every day in the fresh air; seek out-of-door recreations.
✓ Ventilate every room you occupy.
✓ Try to have thorough daily elimination of wastes.
✓ Stand, sit, and walk erectly to maintain good posture.
✓ Keep the teeth, gums, and tongue clean.
✓ Avoid alcohol and tobacco.
✓ Breathe deeply. Keep serene.

HEALTHFUL CHOICES. "An apple a day keeps the doctor away." Indeed, fruit is a valuable food. There are minerals in the body, and as your body works they are used and must be replaced. Both fruits and vegetables help to replace them and to keep the body in good working condition. Rosy cheeks and red lips show that you have good blood, which depends upon a good supply of iron. Strong bones need a supply of lime (calcium), and muscles are kept firm by a fresh supply of iron, phosphorus, and potassium. Fruits and vegetables help to supply these. So it is necessary to use fruits and vegetables every day. Table 2 shows which foods supply which vitamins, so you can be sure to have good nutrition with every meal or snack. And don't forget to drink plenty of water. (Some fruits provide that, too!)

Table 2. Foods That Supply Vitamins

NAME	USE IN THE BODY	FOODS THAT SUPPLY
Vitamin A	To maintain health at all ages and to promote the growth of children	Cod liver oil, liver, milk products, butter, kidney, carrots
Vitamin B_1	To maintain healthy nervous system, aids digestion	Whole-grained cereals, nuts, fruits and vegetables, milk
Vitamin B_2	Important for body growth, utilization of fats, eyes and nails	Milk products, meat, wholemeal cereal, cheese, eggs, liver, green leafy vegetables, whey powder
Vitamin B_3	Helps convert food into energy; helps maintain proper brain function	Whole grains, milk products, meat, poultry, fish, nuts, broccoli, green peas, green beans
Vitamin B_6	Helps produce essential proteins; helps convert protein into energy	Whole wheat products, meat, fish, nuts, green beans, bananas, green leafy vegetables, potatoes
Vitamin B_{12}	Helps convert carbohydrates into energy; maintenance of central nervous system; helps make amino acids	Dairy products, eggs, liver
Vitamin C	For healthy skin, fights cell damage, antioxidant	Citrus fruits, green vegetables, tomatoes
Vitamin D	Helps to build bones and teeth, helps the body absorb calcium	Butter, milk, egg yolks
Vitamin E	Stabilization of the immune system, anti-inflammatory	Sunflowers, avocado, vegetable oils, nuts, flaxseed
Vitamin K	Essential for blood clotting	Dark green leafy vegetables, liver, egg yolks

KEEPING YOUNG WHILE KEEPING HOUSE. Exercise of the various muscles and organs is sometimes the best possible rest. Suppose you find yourself tense and nervous in the midst of a particularly trying day. Sit in a comfortable low chair, close the eyes, let the head relax forward, and banish all troublesome thoughts. Even five minutes spent in this manner will do wonders. Another chair-bound exercise to do for keeping the waist supple: With hands on hips, stretch slowly first to one side and then to the other, until the muscles "pull" and are energized and refreshed. Try it and see how "ready for work" you feel.

Proper posture and breathing (deeply) also strengthen muscles while resting the whole body. Always stand up straight, so that the weight is on the balls of the feet, the chest is raised, and the abdomen held back. This gives the spine the normal double curve, allowing freedom of breathing, proper circulation, and good digestion. This habit of proper standing can be practiced while busy at various household tasks, when answering the doorbell, or at any other time when standing for a few moments. Then try this exercise for additional benefits:

1. Raise arms shoulder high, with palms held forward.
2. Stretch arms outward and push them back as far as possible.
3. Bring arms back to original position.
4. Repeat several times and relax.

REDUCING STRAIN. Modern equipment relieves the strain of heavy housework. The old-time wash basin was attended with backache and arm strain. The new washing machine calls for a normal play of muscles, especially if carried on in an airy, sunny kitchen. Ironing also, if done with up-to-date equipment, gives beneficial light exercise to the arm muscles. Moreover, moderate muscular activity exerted with a definite accomplishment in mind has a psychological effect that is considerable.

SKIN CARE. Do you know how to rouse pale, sallow skins? Do you know what causes blackheads? Do you know why the nose, especially, is apt to have enlarged pores? Your skin is changing every day. As old skin dies, new skin forms to take its place. By the proper treatment, you can make this new skin just what you would love to have. Carry out a facial regimen faithfully, and before long your skin will take on the softness and fine texture that nature intended. Here are some specific treatments:

Removing blackheads: Apply hot cloths to the face until skin is slightly reddened. With a rough washcloth, work up a heavy lather of pure mild soap. Rub into the pores thoroughly—always with an upward and outward motion. Rinse with clear hot water, then with cold. If possible, rub your face for 30 seconds with a lump of ice. Dry carefully.

Reducing pores: Wring a cloth from hot water, lather it with pure mild soap, and apply it to your face. When the heat has expanded the pores, rub in very gently. Repeat this hot water and lather application several times, stopping at once if your skin feels sensitive. Finish by rubbing the skin for 30 seconds with a lump of ice.

Prevent blemishes: One night a week, fill a bowl with hot (almost boiling) water and bend over the top, covering your head with a heavy towel so that no steam can escape. Steam for 30 seconds, and then wash your face as normal.

THE RIGHT WAY TO MANICURE. Cutting the cuticle is ruinous! When you do so, you leave little unprotected places all around the tender nail root. These become rough, sore, and ragged; they grow unevenly and cause painful hangnails. Instead, soften and remove surplus cuticles without knife or scissors by applying moisturizer to the nail base. Gently press back the cuticle. If once or twice each week you take five minutes to manicure, you will never be bothered with coarse, overgrown nails.

KNOW YOUR NEIGHBORHOOD

If you wish to reap the benefits of living in a good neighborhood, you must be a good neighbor. No family or individual has a right to spoil a neighborhood by neglecting the home and yard or by behaving obnoxiously. Even though a person does not know the neighbors, you are obligated to respect the neighbors' rights.

LIVING AMONG OTHERS. Think about what a loss of community services mean. A good water supply, adequate sewerage systems, and good roads are among the community services that the average person regards as necessities. Existence without them seems unthinkable. Yet, community services cannot exist or continue to exist unless the people of the community are interested in having them and will support them. For the maintenance of community services, each individual should (1) vote intelligently, (2) obey laws, and (3) support educational, philanthropic, and religious institutions.

Every individual is in some way dependent upon someone else. It is impossible to make a success unless other people help, and you help others. That is the reason why a family needs help from every member and why a community needs every family to help it.

Each person has community responsibilities, such as:
- ✓ Obey all laws drawn up for your protection.
- ✓ Keep your community clean. Don't be a litterbug.
- ✓ Use with care library books and textbooks entrusted to you.
- ✓ Make use of the facilities provided by your community: libraries, museums, playgrounds, art galleries, and concerts.
- ✓ Help improve the community. Town officials usually welcome the positive interest of citizens in community affairs.

THE ART OF MAKING FRIENDS

Many luxuries we buy with money. Friendship is one of the luxuries we can purchase only with time. Naturally everyone desires friends and everyone needs friends of all ages. Through friendships we develop a sympathetic understanding for one another. If we make friends, we must always be friendly and be true friends.

GETTING TO KNOW YOU. It is good for us if we know various types—some who are vivacious and some who are retiring—because each one gives us something that is worthwhile. Real friendship means having true friends who are friends always and loyal through every kind of experience. Finding new friends and cultivating their friendship is a great joy. Remember these pointers, below.

THESE QUALITIES MAKE YOU LIKEABLE	ARE YOU A GOOD FRIEND?
• Interest in others. • Willingness to go out of your way to help others. • Kindliness—willingness to treat others as you like to be treated. • Flexibility—willingness to "give in." • Dependability—doing what you say you will, showing you can be trusted. • Neatness in personal appearance. • Ability to be a good listener. • Sense of humor.	• Do you listen attentively? • Are you modest? • Do you refrain from talking about yourself most of the time? • Do you give credit to others? • Can you be depended upon to do what you promise? • Are you unselfish with others? • Can you control your temper? • Do you refrain from being sarcastic? • Do you refrain from arguing?

Distinguish between animated discussion and heated argument, and avoid the latter. Always think before you speak.

THE HAPPY WAY OF DOING THINGS

The idea that constant politeness would render social life too stiff and restrained springs from a false estimate of politeness. True politeness is perfect ease and freedom. It simply consists in treating others as you love to be treated yourself. Coarseness and vulgarity are the effects of education and habit; they cannot be charged upon nature. Nature is graceful, and affectation, with all her art, can never produce anything half so pleasing. The very perfection of elegance is to imitate nature as closely as possible; and how much better it is to have the reality than the imitation!

COURTESY AND KINDNESS. The basis of acts of courtesy is consideration for the comfort, the rights, and the feelings of others. This brings happiness to everyone. Courtesy is due the members of the family more than it is due anyone else. A happy life is the desire of every family, and is easily attained if each member is courteous and kind to the others. Do you start the day with a pleasant "Good morning" and a smile? Even if things do seem wrong, smile. Always thank a member  of your family for any courtesy. When asking a favor, "please" brings a much quicker and better result. If you are ever in doubt as to what to do, do what will show consideration for the other's feelings.

A special note for married couples: The happiest married couples are scrupulous in paying to each other a thousand minute attentions, generally thought too trifling to be of any importance. And yet on these very trifles depend their continued love for each other. A birthday present accompanied with a kind word, reserving for each other the most luxurious fruit or most comfortable chair, even the habit of always saying, "Will you have the goodness . . . ?" and "Thank you"—all these seemingly trivial things have a great effect on domestic felicity. Keep the other person in mind at all times.

MANNERS AND ETIQUETTE. Manners and etiquette are similar, yet they differ. *Manners* is the name given to our natural ways of living or acting, in other words our behavior, whereas *etiquette* is the name given to the rules of conduct observed in polite society. By knowing the rules of etiquette, what to do at the proper time and place, we are much helped to develop gracious manners.

The following simple rules will ensure a happy household:

1. Treat each member of your family as you would treat a guest.
2. Respect the personal rights of every member of your family.
3. Be loyal to each one in your family.
4. Be kind and courteous always.
5. Be thoughtful of your elders.
6. Keep the affairs of the household within the home.

A special note about children: As the saying goes, "monkey see, monkey do." Children imitate actions and repeat conversations; they even imitate the mental attitude of the family. Every person living in a home affects the life of the child. This is why an older brother or sister needs to realize that conduct and words, whether good or bad, will be reflected in the younger members. Teach the ideal of character, below. Such an ideal is worthwhile because *behavior* reveals one's *character*.

- Agreeable and cheerful
- Honest and dependable
- Resourceful
- Respectful of others
- Pleasing of voice
- An interesting conversationalist
- Broad-minded and tactful
- Self-controlled
- Cooperative
- Courteous
- Uses proper grammar
- Sociable

RESPECTING ONE'S ELDERS. Nothing tends to foster the genuine politeness that springs from good feeling so much as scrupulous attention to the aged. There is something extremely delightful and salutary in the free and happy intercourse of the old and young. The freshness and enthusiasm of youth cheers the aged; and age can return the benefit a hundredfold, by its mild maxims of experience and wisdom. Youth and age are too much separated; the young flock together, and leave the old to themselves. We seem to act upon the principle that there cannot be sympathy between these two extremes of life, whereas there may be, in fact, a most charming sympathy—a sympathy more productive of mutual benefit than any other in the world. What is there on earth more beautiful than an aged person full of contentment and benevolence!

PRACTICE SELF-DISCIPLINE. "Personal regimen" is a phrase describing the discipline used by an individual to keep oneself clean, well groomed, and cheerful. Think of the word "regiment." Living in a civilized world, in a forward-looking community, and in a respected family requires the observance of certain standards or rules. These relate to desirable traits of character and to cleanliness as well. One's personal regimen is successful only when he or she observes these standards, thereby making them the rule. Don't delay; start one today.

Proper dental care should be part of a daily regimen of good health. Many sicknesses come from poor teeth, and often much money is spent on doctors' bills that can be prevented if the teeth are well cared for.

BEING PART OF A FAMILY

One of the main purposes of a home is to rear children so they will become happy and healthful. Belonging to a family gives one a sense of security by knowing others who live as you do. Each member should do her or her share to make a home. It is not fair for any one member to assume all the responsibility.

A family can be happy with only the necessities of life, and everyone working together and for one another. Luxury does not provide happiness, for luxury cannot buy health and contentment. Often when a family has too many luxuries, selfishness finds a way into family life, and that only leads to grief and strife.

THE REARING OF CHILDREN. It is beyond all doubt that the state of a mother affects her child. Therefore, the first rule, and the most important of all, in education is that a mother govern  her own feelings and keep her heart and conscience pure. Gentleness, patience, and love are almost everything in education, especially to those helpless little creatures who have just entered into the world where everything is new and strange. Gentleness is a sort of mild atmosphere, and it enters into a child like the sunshine into the rose-bud, slowly but surely expanding it into beauty and vigor.

Like adults, babies grow better if they have systematic care and a definite time for everything—for feeding, for bathing, for sleeping. Feeding time is most important of all, and each day you should have a plan for the child's waking and sleeping hours. Following is more information for each part of this routine.

FEEDING. Although the very best infant food is the mother's milk, it is not always possible for a mother to nurse her baby. Formula must then be provided. Be sure the milk or formula is fresh, and the utensils clean and sterilized. For bottle feeding, warm the milk to body temperature by setting the bottle in warm water just before feeding.

BATHING. Have the room free from drafts. The water should be warm. Have near at hand the small tub of water, washcloths, soft towels, gentle soap, powder, cotton swabs, and the baby's clean clothes ready to slip on.

Before undressing the baby, cleanse the nostrils and ears (outside only). Wash the face and scalp with soap and water. Then quickly soap and rinse the body, keeping the back well-supported. After removal from the tub, lay the baby on a blanket and pat the skin dry. Put on the diaper and clothing with as little motion as possible; let the baby lie on the lap (until he is old enough to sit on his own) and draw the clothing up over his feet.

SLEEPING. A baby requires more sleep than older members of a family, and so should sleep in a room of his own. If the baby cannot have a separate room, he must have a bed of his own. Put the baby to sleep at regular times each day, and allow the proper amount of rest.

OTHER BASIC NEEDS AND GUIDANCE. After a baby is three weeks old, he should be outside every day unless the weather is unpleasant. Clothe the baby properly for both indoor and outdoor activities. Plan the clothing for comfort, which demands that it be durable, simple in design, and allowing of freedom of movement.

During infancy and the preschool period, a child makes his or her most rapid growth and forms habits of character and health. Since a baby or little child is too young to realize what is best, guidance is necessary. Remember to teach that the only sure way, as well as the easiest, to *appear* good is to *be* good. Table 3 should aid in passing on the best possible habits. Teach children well, and they will reward you.

Table 3. Teaching a Child Good Habits

HABITS OF EATING	HABITS OF CLEANLINESS	HABITS OF EXERCISE	HABITS OF REST
• Eat a variety of foods. • Eat proper foods not foods of their own choosing. • Eat plenty of fruits and vegetables every day. • Eat slowly and chew thoroughly. • Eat at regular hours • Drink at least six glasses of water daily.	• Take a bath every day or at least every other day. • Brush the teeth at least twice a day. See a dentist at least twice a year. • Keep the hands and face clean. • Wash the hands before and after eating. • Change all underclothing often, and always after each bath. • Have a regular bowel movement daily. • Cover the mouth and nose when coughing or sneezing.	• Play outside every day. • Have plenty of fresh air always. Live outside in the sunshine as much as possible. • Sit, stand, and walk properly to develop a correct posture.	• Rest a while each day in the afternoon. • Go to bed early at a regular hour every evening and secure ten or more hours of sleep.

HABITS OF CLOTHING	HABITS OF KINDNESS AND COURTESY	HABITS OF CONDUCT	HABITS OF PLAY
• Wear clean, healthful, and comfortable underclothing. • Put on clothing and fasten it. • Hang up clothing and put away accessories.	• Be kind to parents and all other persons. • Help others. • Be courteous to everyone.	• Carry out ideas if at all possible. • Work or play without interruption. • Talk in a natural way. • Obey with no thoughts of fear.	• Play well with other children. • Select interesting toys. • Put away toys after playing.

BEDSIDE MANNERS

There are many cases of illness not serious enough to make it necessary to send the patient to the hospital, yet in which the patient must stay in bed and have good care. In such cases, someone in the home must do the nursing and should have some knowledge of such work.

INVALID COOKERY. One of the most important things for the home nurse to know is how to prepare and serve the food the patient needs. Food is especially important, because a poorly nourished body cannot resist nor overcome disease, and in many cases regulating the diet is the main treatment. For special diets of this sort, the home nurse will follow carefully the doctor's instructions regarding kind, amount, and preparation of food.

In preparing any food for a sick person, try to do so even more carefully than when it is to be served to others. The dainty appearance of food is a very important factor and often makes one willing to eat who otherwise might not be able to do so.

The preparation of a food tray will be much appreciated by the sick person who is not well enough to come to table. The tray should be made attractive, with clean cloth or doilies and dishes that look well together. Nicked or cracked dishes should not be used if there are others to be had. Try to think of all of the utensils that are needed to eat what is served so that the person will not have

Take great care when preparing a tray for someone who is not feeling well.

to ask for anything. Butter, sugar, and salt should not be forgotten if they are to be used, and a glass of cold water is nearly always desired. Try to keep hot food hot by having the dishes warmed and the food covered. After all your trouble, do not feel bad if the food you have served is not eaten. Sick people have whimsical tastes, and well people must be patient with them.

Diets for the sick may be classified in the following ways:
1. *Liquid*, including broths, milk, gruels, cream soups, etc.
2. *Soft*, including soft-cooked eggs, milk toast, jellies, etc.
3. *Soft solid*, including eggs, creamed toast, asparagus, baked custards, tender chicken, oysters, creamed sweetbreads, etc.
4. *Special diet*, one ordered by a physician for a particular case.

OVERCOMING A SICKNESS. Sometimes, in spite of ourselves, we do get sick. If you catch a cold or flu, try the recipes below as well as these suggestions that may help to cure it.
+ Take a hot bath and go to bed. This will keep you warm, protect you from drafts, and prevent other people from catching your cold.
+ Drink plenty of water.
+ Take only easily digested food, with a generous amount of liquids.
+ Be sure that the bowels move regularly.
+ If your cold does not respond to home treatment or is accompanied by a severe cough, consult a doctor.

Milk Toast

Arrange 2 slices of toast in a hot dish and pour over them 1 cup hot milk, to which 2 tsp butter and ½ tsp salt have been added.

Hot Lemonade

Wash and wipe a lemon. Cut a thin slice from the middle and squeeze the rest into a bowl. Put in 2 tbs sugar or honey, pour on ¾ cup boiling water, and strain into a cup. Serve with the slice of lemon on top.

"The well-being of an individual depends upon the food that she takes. Her home may be poor, her clothes scanty, but food she must have."

Kitchen
Arts
and Sciences

The *art of cookery* is a late development, consequent on culture and the increase of wealth. It is inextricably bound up with the necessities of nutrition, but mere hunger will not produce cookery. Cooking itself has often been looked upon as a despised work. In late years, happily, with the rise of science, a new interest in the subject has been awakened, and women of education and attainments have become more generally concerned with what is going on with their kitchens.

It is essential that every housekeeper should know something of the scientific principles of nutrition and should endeavor to have the meals served in her household be both wholesome and attractive. If we are "but what we eat," we are also the product of all the influences that play about us as we eat. As Dr. Harvey W. Wiley, for many years chief chemist of the U.S. Department of Agriculture stated, "The study of buying for the table and the proper preparation of what is bought is as much an art as the . . . composition of a fine piece of poetry." If the wise housekeeper is skillful in preparing the various foodstuffs in appetizing ways, the daily menu will be both adequate and pleasing.

FOOD AND ITS USES

In many ways, the body is like a machine, with food as its source of motive energy. The body differs from the machine, however, in that the food or fuel assists in building up as well as in supplying energy. Further, if more fuel is taken into the body than is necessary, it can be stored as reserve material, usually in the form of fat.

MENU PLANNING. A variety of foods is necessary to keep the body in a normal condition, and nature has laid the foundation of a science that is rapidly developing as the result of careful and painstaking laboratory study. The scientist has classified the substances that make up our foods under five heads:

Water — Enters every tissue, regulates body temperature, and has a part to play in all muscular work.

Minerals — Active in body building in chemical reactions. *Sources:* Spinach, peas, lettuce, potatoes, turnips, apples, oranges, berries.

Protein — Builds and repairs tissue and it may yield energy. *Sources:* Lean of meats, dairy, dried legumes (beans, lentils), nuts.

Carbohydrates — Starches and sugars; yield energy. *Sources:* Cereals (bread, flour), pasta, rice, sugar, honey, jellies, dried fruits.

Fats — Yield energy. *Sources:* Butter, cream, lard, pork, chocolate.

When food-buying, the money should be divided and spent as follows:

1. One part or more for vegetables and fruit.
2. One part or more for milk, cheese, and eggs.
3. One part or less for meat and fish.
4. One part or more for bread and cereals.
5. One part or less for sugar, tea, coffee, chocolate, and flavoring.

RULES FOR BUILDING MENUS. To plan a daily menu that will provide the kind and amount of food required by each member of the family is the most important part of the homemaker's duties, and requires much time, thought, and a knowledge of foods. To plan for the day's meals as a unit or even a week at a time is much better than to plan for each separate meal. The menu builder must have a general idea of the classes of food and the specific functions of food in the  body, together with a knowledge of the food and energy requirements of each member of her family. These rules should help.

- Try to serve some food from each group of food at each meal.
- Serve fresh vegetables every day of the year if possible. Include in each meal the foods that are needed by each member of the family.
- Serve easily digested foods for children and old people. Serve the hearty energy food for active adults.
- Simple, well-cooked foods are better than elaborate dishes.
- Serve a few dishes at one meal and see that no one food class predominates. For example, potatoes and rice are both starchy foods and nearly equivalent. One is sufficient at a meal.
- Carbohydrate foods should have both starches and sugar well represented, with more starch than sugar.
- There is no connection between nutritive value and price of food.

 To make sure that you are using foods that help you to look and feel your best, you need to think of all the foods you eat during the entire day. Hence, menus for the three meals of a day should be planned together.

WELL-BALANCED MEALS AND BUDGETS. Every intelligent person should understand the essentials of a good diet, and should aim to eat well-balanced meals. In planning menus, perhaps the most important point to consider is to serve a well-balanced menu that is within the food allowance that the homemaker can afford (see Table 4). If the amount the homemaker budgets for the week's food supply is sufficient to allow a few of the more expensive foods, they should not all be included on one menu, or on the menus of one day, but should be distributed over the week. Then, again, careful planning of the week's food supply can result in meals that are not only nutritionally correct and reasonable in price, but ones that give pleasure and satisfaction. With some forethought, the homemaker can also plan menus that do not require unnecessary work and time.

Some suggestions are given here for helping you in menu planning.

- Plan meals for an entire day or for several days.
- The most desirable diet contains milk, butter, whole cereals, fresh vegetables, green leafy vegetables, and eggs.
- Use foods on hand, or left-overs, attractively served (see page 56).
- Select foods of contrasting flavors and variations (see page 36).
- Combine moist and dry foods in each meal.
- Use sweet foods at the end of the meal.
- Include plenty of milk in cooking as well as for drinking.
- Plan how to serve the meal attractively.

 To plan menus quickly, it is helpful to refer to lists of different kinds of foods—soup lists, meat lists, vegetable lists, and so on. If you have a recipe card file, list foods belonging to the same groups on cards of the file.

Table 4. Planning Diets by the Yardstick of Your Budget

FOODS	LOW COST	MODERATE	LIBERAL
A. MILK			
• As beverage • As cheese • In cooked food	3 to 4 cups a day, each child; 2 to 3 cups a day, each adult	4 cups a day, each child; 3 cups a day, each adult	4 cups a day, each child; 3 to 4 cups a day, each adult
B. VEGETABLES AND FRUITS			
• Potatoes and sweet potatoes	2 servings a day	1 or 2 servings a day	1 serving a day
• Dry beans, peas, peanuts, nuts	4 times a week	2 or 3 times a week	1 serving a week
• Tomatoes, citrus fruits or other vitamin C-rich food	5 servings a week; 1 serving a day, children under 4	5 or 6 servings a week	2 servings a day
• Leafy, green, yellow vegetables	6 servings a week	1 or 2 servings a day	1 or 2 servings a day
• Other vegetables and fruits	6 servings a week	2 servings a day	2 or 3 servings a day
C. EGGS	3 or 4 a week, each person	5 or 6 a week, each person	1 a day, sometimes 2, each person
D. LEAN MEAT, FISH, POULTRY	5 or 6 servings a week	7 or 8 servings a week	1 serving a day, often 2 servings
E. OTHER FOODS	Cereal daily Bread, every meal Dessert, 1 daily (if desired)	Cereal daily Bread, every meal Dessert, 1 daily (if desired)	Wide variety of cereals, breads, other baked goods Desserts

In well-planned menus, there are foods that form contrast in:

- *Flavor.* Some have a pronounced flavor, others have a bland flavor.
- *Dryness and moistness.* Some foods are dry, some are moist. Both kinds should appear on a well-balanced menu.
- *Color.* There should be a mixture of white or light-colored foods with those of deeper colors.
- *Temperature.* Hot foods (at least one) and cold foods help to make a meal palatable.
- *Size or shape.* A mixture of foods of different-sized pieces or shapes adds to the attractiveness of a meal.

A well-balanced meal contains foods from each group,
plus a healthful beverage.

Finished menus should be tested to see if they meet all these requirements:

✓ Is it suited to the needs of each member of the family?
✓ Is it within the income and allowance?
✓ Is there a good distribution of soft and solid food?
✓ Does the week's menu offer variety from day to day?
✓ Does it call for simple table service and preparation of dishes?

DAILY MEALS

Meals should be served regularly for good health and comfort, and both hot and cold foods should be included in a menu. Each meal is important for special reasons, and all should be enjoyed.

BREAKFAST. There are several good reasons why the family should all have breakfast. First, the body is like an automobile; both must be kept going. To do so, the body needs fuel in the form of food. Second, there is a longer time between the evening meal and breakfast than between any other two meals. The body needs food after its long fast. Third, headaches, irritability, and other annoying conditions of the body may arise from going without breakfast. For a simple breakfast, choose fruit, cereal, lightly buttered toast, and a beverage. For a heavier meal, add egg, bacon, and a muffin.

LUNCH. Luncheon dishes should be simple and easily prepared. Foods that can be carried in a lunchbox are limited in kind and number. Sandwiches are the basis of most box lunches.

Suggestions for sandwich fillings are:
- Peanut butter with honey, or coconut, or crushed bananas.
- Chopped dates or raisins with nuts, moistened with lemon or orange juice.
- Raisins and nuts chopped fine and moistened with grape juice.
- Cold chicken or lobster, chopped, seasoned, and moistened with lemon juice or salad dressing.

For variety or an extra nibble, tuck into the lunchbox a few salted nuts, raisins, figs, stuffed dates, or a bar of milk chocolate.

Standards for sandwichery: A well-made sandwich requires slices of bread with butter or dressing, such as mayonnaise. Its purpose is to make the sandwich taste better, to add nutritive value, and to prevent a juice filling from soaking into the bread. It should have a flavorful filling that is not heaped in the center, does not fall out at the edges, and is easy to bite through. Lastly, a well-made sandwich is not dry and curling at the edges.

Ideas for cutting sandwiches.

DINNER. What shall we have for dinner? That question is asked in thousands of homes daily. It's an important question, too, and must be answered wisely by every homemaker. Dinner is for most families the largest meal of the day, so it pays to plan the menu economically. The following plans provide a guideline for a range of budgets.

PLAIN DINNER	ELABORATE DINNER	FORMAL DINNER
Main Course *(meat or fish)* Vegetables Bread and butter Salad or dessert	Appetizer *(clear soup)* Main course *(meat or fish)* Vegetables Bread and butter Salad and/or dessert	Appetizer *(consommé)* Main Course *(meat)* Vegetables Rolls Salad Dessert

ECONOMIC SHOPPING

In order that food be pleasing, it is not necessary that it be expensive. The larger part of the price of costlier foods is paid for appearance, flavor, or scarcity. And while people who can afford them may be justified in buying, it is well to remember that the cheaper foods frequently contain as much if not more nutriment and, with a little care, can be made just as pleasing. It is the lazy and unskilled cook who pays exorbitant prices for food rather than taking the trouble to make the common foodstuffs appeal to the palate.

A TRIP TO THE MARKET. If all women would insist upon clean markets, grocery stores, bakeries, and meat shops, it would not take long to bring about more sanitary conditions in many of them. It is not necessary to go to market every day; two or three trips a week should be enough. One should make a list of things needed and try to save time and effort by purchasing all the necessary articles at one time and in one place, or in the same neighborhood if possible. It is well too, occasionally, to weigh the contents of packages put up by manufacturers to see how they compare in price with the same amount bought in bulk. Package goods usually cost more than goods bought in bulk. Extra glass, tin, paper, and baskets must be paid for.

"READY-TO-EAT," BULK FOODS, AND OTHER RULES FOR SAVING. One point worth mentioning is that "ready-to-eat" foods, except perhaps in the case of cereals, are expensive and not always so good as the old-fashioned dishes prepared in the old-fashioned way. Also, except for fruit and vegetables, which will be used at once, food should not be bought in small amounts; food in bulk is usually cheaper.

Another way to save is by buying less-tender and cheaper cuts of meat (see pages 46 and 47 for popular cuts). It also pays to consider the amount of waste in meat, such as the bone in many cuts. These are minor matters, but they all play their part in economical living.

Here are additional suggestions for good shopping:

- Avoid food put in fancy packages, such as nuts in small glass jars.
- Buy in large packages except when the food may deteriorate if the package stands open.
- Remember that uncooked foods are always less expensive than the ready cooked.
- Know the prevailing market prices and quality of foods that you wish to purchase.
- Avoid handling food. Fresh fruit and vegetables, such as pears, plums, and tomatoes, may be bruised and will spoil.
- Remember that out-of-season foods are always expensive.
- Make a study of sizes, brands, and grades in order that you may get the best value for your money.
- Do not follow fads or fancies in foods. Always choose foods that provide the most nutrition.
- Remember to satisfy aesthetic demands, too. Food must be enjoyed in order to be thoroughly digested.

AVOIDING FOOD WASTE

Tossing pennies into the garbage can or pouring nectar down the drain pipe of the sink would be unthinkable waste. Nevertheless, solid foods that cost money are often thrown into the garbage can, and nourishing liquids are poured into the sink. Let us consider some common food wastes and ways of avoiding them.

Vegetable and fruit parings: All fruits and vegetables should be pared as thinly as possible. This will effect a great saving as well as conserve their vitamin and mineral value.

Vegetable water: Cook vegetables in as little water as possible.

Bacon fat: Since it has the decided flavor of bacon, it cannot be used in dishes requiring bland fats, such as a fruit pie crust. But it can be used in the crust of meat pies.

Stale and dry bread: What shall I do with bread crusts or bread too stale for table use? That is a question that perplexes the home manager who strives to cut down food wastes to a minimum. There are many recipes containing bread or crumbs, including those in the chart below.

STALE BREAD	SOFT BREAD CRUMBS	DRIED BREAD CRUMBS
Toast	Scalloped or au gratin	Dipping croquettes
French toast	dishes	Scalloped dishes using
Soft breads	Macaroni and cheese	moist food
Soup topper	Stuffing	Puddings
	Meatloaf	

 It is thrifty to buy day-old bread, which usually sells for less than the fresh product.

THE SCIENCE OF COOKING

The importance of good cooking cannot be overestimated. Cooking destroys many germs and that is one reason why some cooked foods are better and more wholesome than uncooked ones. Cooking has other important purposes, too: it renders food more capable of mastication and consequently of digestion. It does this both by changing its actual structure and by making it more appetizing, thus stimulating the flow of the saliva and gastric juices. The careful cooking and serving of food are themselves the result of a developed aesthetic sense, and are at the same time a means of further development.

The well-being of an individual depends upon the food that she takes. Her home may be poor, her clothes scanty, but food she must have. Food produces energy and furnishes the materials for growth. But how much food do we need?

THE COUNTING OF CALORIES. When we think of the value of food to the body, we must think in terms of heat or energy. Food produces heat, and this heat is set free in the body and becomes the source of power or energy.

Scientists have found a way of measuring the amount of heat or energy the body requires to do its work. They have also found out how much heat given amounts of food produce when burned. When we measure heat, we use the calorie. A calorie is the amount of heat necessary to raise one pound (about a pint) of water four degrees Fahrenheit. Men, women, girls, and boys need different amounts of calories daily, depending upon their size, shape, age, and amount of work they do. A great many foods have been analyzed and many lists of 100-calorie portions have been prepared. By becoming familiar with the lists and taking a little trouble to figure, you can know in a general way whether or not you are eating enough. Table 5 (opposite) will help you select suitable foods and amounts.

Table 5. 100-Calorie Portions of Some Commonly Used Foods

FRUITS	
Apple or banana or orange	1 large
Dates	4
Figs, dried	2
Raisins	25 or 30
VEGETABLES	
Asparagus, canned	20 to 25 stalks
Lettuce	1 large head, 1¼ lb.
Peas, canned	1 cup drained
Potatoes	1 medium
Spinach	4 qt.
Tomatoes, fresh	1 lb.
Turnips	2 to 3 medium
CEREAL AND BREAD	
Bread, white	1 slice, ½ inch thick
Corn flakes	1¼ cupfuls
Crackers, Graham	8 2-inch squares
Cream of wheat	¼ cupful
Flour	¼ cupful
Macaroni	¼ cup
Rice, dry	2 tablespoonfuls
BUILDING FOODS	
Cheese	1 oz.
Eggs	1½ (an egg yields about 67 calories)
Milk	⅝ cupful
Round steak, medium fat	2 oz.
Oysters	10 to 12
FATS	
Butter	1 tablespoonful
Cream, medium	2 tablespoonfuls
Olive oil	1 tablespoonful
SWEETS	
White sugar	2 level tablespoonfuls
Molasses	1 tablespoonful

THE HANDLING OF MEAT

Whether or not meat is absolutely essential to the human body has never been adequately worked out, but there is flavor in the so-called "extractives" of meat that nothing can altogether replace, no matter how firmly we may be convinced that other foods contain as much or more protein or fats. The cooking of meats is important, for good cooking enhances and poor cooking lessens or destroys meat's nutritive value. Cooking develops a pleasing taste and odor and loosens the proteins of the connective tissues, thus making meat more tender. Extreme heat, however, tends to harden the albumin of the lean portions and to weaken the flavor of the extractives.

Meat is, in most households, the most expensive food placed upon the table but not always the richest from the physiological standpoint. It behooves the householder to buy wisely and to consider the suggestions here for cooking the cheaper cuts of meat. A handy timetable can be found on page 48.

COOKING TENDER MEAT. Roasting, broiling, and pan-broiling develop a rich flavor in meat and are the most popular methods. Only choice, tender cuts can be cooked in these ways, because dry heat or hot fat toughens meat.

COOKING TOUGH MEAT. The cheaper cuts have a great deal of connective tissue that makes the meat tough. The greater part of the animal yields tough meats that are juicy and contain excellent food value. Slow cooking in water for a long time softens the meat fibers and dissolves the connective tissue, making the meat more tender. In order to tenderize tough meats and obtain the rich flavor of browned meat, they are chopped, pounded, pressed, or cubed to break or weaken the fibers, and then the meat is suitable to broil, pan-broil, or roast.

The next page presents helpful descriptions of ways to prepare less-than-choice cuts for the frugal homekeeper.

Roasting: The chief point to remember is that meat should be quickly browned so that the crust formed may retain the juices. The oven should be hot when meat is put in; then heat is gently reduced.

Braising: A cross between boiling and baking; one of the best methods of cooking large pieces of tough lean meat. (See the recipe below.)

Broiling: Its object is to coagulate all the albumin on meat's surface, sealing pores so that no juices escape. Meat cooked by this method is more wholesome that if prepared in any other way.

Frying: Cooking in very hot fat. The secret of success is to have fat hot enough to harden meat's surface immediately and deep enough to cover it. Since fat can be saved and used many times, use of a large quantity is not extravagant.

Sautéing: Commonly called frying; consists of cooking with a little fat in a shallow pan. Can make articles greasy; use with caution, and employ butter, olive oil, or a cheaper fat.

Stewing: Cooking in a little liquid in a covered vessel over the fire. Thickening and vegetables are usually added. Cut meat in small pieces and brown; add boiling liquid and cook a few minutes. Reduce heat and cook very slowly.

Braised Steak

1½ lbs. round or shoulder steak	1 tsp. salt
4 tbs. flour	pepper to taste
fat trimmed from meat	hot water, about ¼ cup

Wipe the steak. Remove fat. Slash the edges to prevent curling. Cut the meat into about 6 pieces. Put the flour, salt, and pepper on a plate. Mix. Then roll the meat in the flour mixture. Cut the fat trimmed from the meat in small pieces. Put it in a heavy frying pan over a low flame. Brown meat in the fat. After browning, add water. Cover. Place the pan over the simmering burner. Continue cooking for 1½ hours or more, until the steak is tender. Serve hot on a platter.

KNOW YOUR MEAT

Meat is the flesh of any animals used as food. Good meat must come from a healthy animal. A well-fed animal gives a better grade of meat then a poorly fed one. (This applies to a chicken as well as to a large beef creature.) The tests for good meat are: little or no odor, uniform color, firm to the touch, not moist.

Since meat is one of the most expensive foods, and since it has a very important place in the diet, it is necessary to know how to purchase meat intelligently and prepare it properly. The loin of any animal is usually the best (and most expensive) cut. It is thrifty to buy the less-tender cuts; they can be made very tasty. The following charts explain the various cuts and provide economical preparation suggestions.

Pork Cuts

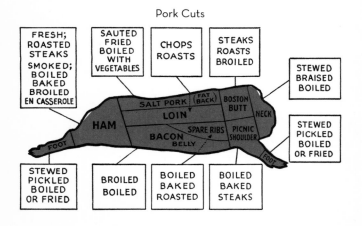

Beef Cuts

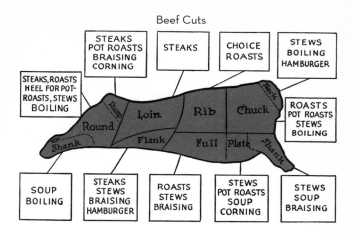

STEAKS
POT ROASTS
BRAISING
CORNING

STEAKS

CHOICE
ROASTS

STEWS
BOILING
HAMBURGER

STEAKS, ROASTS
HEEL FOR POT-
ROASTS, STEWS
BOILING

ROASTS
POT ROASTS
STEWS
BOILING

Rump · Loin · Rib · Chuck · Neck
Round · Flank · Full · Plate · Shank
Shank

SOUP
BOILING

STEAKS
STEWS
BRAISING
HAMBURGER

ROASTS
STEWS
BRAISING

STEWS
POT ROASTS
SOUP
CORNING

STEWS
SOUP
BRAISING

Lamb Cuts

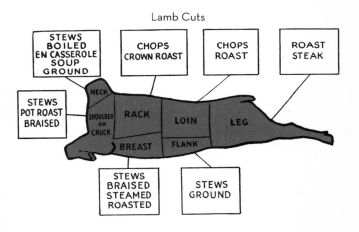

STEWS
BOILED
EN CASSEROLE
SOUP
GROUND

CHOPS
CROWN ROAST

CHOPS
ROAST

ROAST
STEAK

STEWS
POT ROAST
BRAISED

NECK
SHOULDER
OR
CHUCK · RACK · LOIN · LEG
BREAST · FLANK

STEWS
BRAISED
STEAMED
ROASTED

STEWS
GROUND

Table 6. Timetable for Cooking Meats

TYPE OF MEAT	COOKING TIME
Braising *(Suitable for less tender cuts of meat and fowl)*	
Pot roasts	3 to 4 hours
Steaks	1 to 3 hours
Fowl	2 to 3 hours
Broiling *(Suitable for tender slices of beef, lamb, ham, fish)*	
Beefsteaks, 1 inch, rare	8 to 10 minutes each side
Lamb chops, 1 inch, well done	10 to 15 minutes each side
Fish steaks or fillets	10 to 15 minutes on each side
Roasting *(Suitable for tender beef cuts, veal, lamb, fresh pork, ham, chicken, fish)*	
Beef	
. . . rare	16 to 33 minutes per pound; internal temperature 140°F
. . . medium	22 to 45 minutes per pound; internal temperature 160°F
. . . well-done	30 to 50 minutes per pound; internal temperature 170°F
Veal (300° F)	25 to 40 minutes per pound
Lamb (300°F)	30 to 45 minutes per pound; internal temperature 175° to 182°F
Fresh pork (350°F)	Cook fat side up, 30 to 50 minutes per pound; internal temperature 185°F
Ham (300° F) (Bake rind side up) . . . whole (10 to 12 pounds) . . . cottage butt (2 to 4 pounds)	25 minutes per pound. 35 minutes per pound
Chicken 4 to 5 pounds (350°F)	1½ to 2½ hours
Turkey (stuffed) . . . 8 to 14 pounds (325° F)	3 to 4 hours
Fish (375° to 400°F) . . . fillet (3 pounds) . . . whole (4 pounds)	½ hour ½ to ¾ hour

MEAT SUBSTITUTES

In the majority of households, meat is still the central article of every meal; but there is an almost universal desire to decrease the amount of meat consumed, if not totally to eliminate it from the diet. The desire arises partly from the thirst for variety, partly from reasons of economy, and partly from a growing distaste for animal food.

DRIED PEAS AND LENTILS. Nearly everyone is acquainted with baked beans, but how many people know dried peas and lentils as well? In many ways, these dried seeds are good substitutes for meat. They cost much less than meat per pound and have a higher fuel value.

NUTS. Nuts may also be used in place of meat. Ordinarily they are used for dessert or are eaten between meals, and their real food value is never appreciated. They contain a high percentage each of protein, fat, and carbohydrate, and while they differ in composition, nuts in general contain enough protein to take the place of meat. Chopped nuts used in salads or desserts offer variety. Nut butter (see recipe, below) on sandwiches or made into cream soup is palatable and wholesome.

Nut Butter

2 c. unsalted cashews or almonds
3 tbs. vegetable oil

1 tsp. honey
¼ teaspoon salt

Process nuts, 2 tablespoons oil, salt, and sugar or honey 30 seconds. Puree to spreading consistency, adding remaining oil if needed. Store in an airtight container in the refrigerator.

FISH AND POULTRY

The term *fish* includes, besides the fish proper, many other water animals, such as oysters, clams, lobsters, shrimps, and terrapin. In general, fish contains the same kind of nutrients as other food materials, serving the two-fold purpose of tissue-building and production of heat and energy. It is not so rich in nutrients or fuel value as meat, but furnishes an economical source of nitrogen and lends to the diet that variety which is almost essential.

Poultry is the name given to domestic birds suitable for food, such as chicken, turkey, goose, and duck. *Spring chickens* are those about five months old. A chicken over a year old is called a *fowl*. (Note that poultry has a better flavor when full-grown than when too young.) Poultry are fairly rich in nutritive value and wherever possible should be introduced into the menu—for the sake of variety if nothing else. Because the flavor of chicken is so popular, and because it blends well with that of bland foods, it is often combined with other food materials, such as rice, noodles, eggs, and bread. With these combinations, the flavor of the chicken is extended and the cost of the dish is reduced.

SELECTING AND COOKING FISH. Fish spoil readily. In fact, changes causing spoilage take place more rapidly in fish than in any other food. Tests for freshness are: (1) flesh firm and elastic, (2) eyes bright, not sunken, (3) gills not much discolored, (4) scales somewhat firmly attached, not very easily removed, (5) odor fishy but not disagreeable. Decomposition can often be recognized by the odor of the fish or by the test of laying the fish in water. Those that sink may be considered undecomposed and wholesome; those that float, unfit for use. Also, if the eyes have lost their sheen or the cornea is cloudy, or if the meat is so soft that when pressed the indentation of the finger remains, it should be considered unfit for food.

Because fish contains only a small amount of connective tissue, it is not tough and may be baked or broiled in an uncovered pan like tender cuts of meat. Fish may be cooked in water. To prevent it from falling apart, it may be tied loosely in cheesecloth.

SELECTING AND COOKING POULTRY. When choosing fowl for consumption, pay attention to these characteristics: the bird should be short and plump in proportion to its weight; the skin should be clear and smooth; the legs should be smooth, the toes pliable; and there should be a large amount of meat on the breast. A spring chicken should be chosen for broiling; a young chicken for roasting. Capons are considered the choicest of poultry, and cock turkeys are usually considered better than turkeys. The following are two techniques commonly used with poultry.

Trussing: Before roasting a chicken or turkey, it is necessary to truss it. Press the thighs and wings close against the body; fasten securely with skewers and tie with string. Draw the skin of the neck to the back and fasten it.

Stuffing: Use enough stuffing to fill the bird but do not pack it tightly or the stuffing will be soggy. Close the small openings with a skewer; sew the larger one with linen thread and a long needle. Remove skewers and strings before serving.

The heart, liver, and gizzard constitute the giblets, to which the neck is often added. These may be eaten but are more commonly used for making stock.

VEGETABLES

If we want the members of our families to eat more vegetables, we must know how to make them appetizing. The addition of milk, butter, egg, or cheese in the form of good sauces often makes them more palatable and, too, gives added food value. We also need to know how to cook them properly to save nutrients.

CAUTIOUS COOKING. The changes that take place in the cooking of vegetables are briefly these: The cellular tissue is softened and loosened; the nitrogenous substances are coagulated; the starch granules absorb moisture, swell, and burst; and the flavor is developed. The food is rendered more digestible and in most cases more palatable. Overcooking, however, changes and toughens the texture, destroys the coloring matter, and injures the flavor.

Vegetables and Some of Their Nutrients

PROTEINS	CARBOHYDRATES	IRON
Dried peas	Lima beans	Dried beans and peas
Dried beans	Potatoes (all types)	Lima beans
Lentils	Parsnips	Spinach
	Peas	Lettuce
	Corn	String beans
	Beets	Cabbage
	Carrots	Potatoes

COOKING METHODS. There are three common ways: cooking in water, steaming, or baking. On the whole, the simpler methods of preparing are preferred, in the majority of cases bringing the food to its most digestible form. Cook vegetables until they are more tender than when raw but still have a little of the crispness. This is one of the most important points in preserving nutrients and color and in making vegetables tasty. Remember to always wash your vegetables before cooking them.

When choosing a cooking method, remember these points:

- Baking saves minerals. The skin of such vegetables as potatoes prevents oxidation and thus helps to retain vitamin C, but high temperature and long baking may destroy vitamins.
- Steaming causes only a slight loss of minerals. But if cooked for a long time, some vitamins are destroyed.
- Cooking in much water dissolves some of the minerals and vitamins. To save these nutrients, the cooking water should be used for soup, sauce, gravy, or liquid for meat loaf. Cooking in a small amount of water means little loss of nutrients, especially if no water needs to be drained away.

Timetable for Cooking Vegetables

VEGETABLES	MINUTES	VEGETABLES	MINUTES
Asparagus	10 to 30	Kale	10 to 20
Beans, lima, green	20 to 30	Peas, green	8 to 20
Beans, snap, green	15 to 30	Spinach	3 to 10
Beet greens	5 to 15	Squash, Hubard	20 to 30
Broccoli	8 to 20	Squash, summer	10 to 20
Cabbage, green	10 to 15	Potatoes, whole	25 to 35
Carrots, whole	20 to 30	Potatoes, quartered	15 to 25

Vegetables that form in heads (cauliflower, cabbage, etc.) should be soaked, heads down, in salted water to which a few teaspoons of vinegar may be added. Any worms will then crawl out.

CEREALS. Cereals, or grains, are the seeds of grasses that are used for food. (They are named after Ceres, the goddess whom the ancients believed watched over harvests.) Cereals hold an important place in the diet, ranking first among the vegetable foods. They are, moreover, easily prepared, are both palatable and digestible, and are easily preserved without deterioration.

Some people think of "breakfast food" when the word *cereal* is used, but it should not be applied to breakfast cereals only since many other food products are made from the same grains. Flour, vermicelli, macaroni, cornstarch, glucose, corn syrup, and many other commonly used foods are all made from cereals or the grains of certain grasses.

Cereals contain all of the different food classes, but are especially rich in starch. Whole-grain cereals contain an abundance of vitamins, minerals, and cellulose. Because cereals are very dry, hard, and compact, they require long cooking in a large quantity of water. During the cooking process, the cellulose softens and the starch cells swell and burst. It is best to cook cereals in a double boiler. See the timetable below for cooking methods and approximate times.

Timetable for Cooking Cereals

CEREAL	AMOUNT OF WATER	AMOUNT OF SALT	COOKING TIME
1 c. Rolled Oats	2 c.	1 tsp.	30–60 mins.
1 c. Coarse Oatmeal	5 c.	1½ tsp.	4 or more hours
1 c. Cream of Wheat	4–5 c.	1½ tsp.	30–60 mins.
1 c. Cornmeal	5 c.	1½ tsp.	2 hours
1 c. Cracked Wheat	4 c.	1½ tsp.	4 or more hours

POTATOES. Potatoes are more commonly used than other vegetables because they are inexpensive, easily kept, and in season throughout the year. Potatoes are nourishing and easily digested. They can be cooked in a variety of ways, and as they are bland in flavor and neutral in color, they blend well with other foods. Potatoes with smooth skins and no green spots should be selected, and they should be uniform in shape and size. They may be prepared in a variety of ways, but the recipes below are most popular.

Boiled Potatoes

Cook potatoes in boiling salted water until tender (about 30 minutes). Drain and shake in an uncovered saucepan over the fire to dry off any moisture. Cover with a clean folded cloth and keep in a warm place. Remove skins and sprinkle with salt before serving.

Riced Potatoes

Remove skins from hot boiled potatoes or hot baked potatoes and place them, one at a time, in the potato ricer. Press into a heated vegetable dish. Sprinkle with salt and paprika. Garnish with parsley and serve immediately.

Baked Potatoes

Wash the potatoes and wipe dry. If a soft skin is desired, brush the potatoes with oil. Bake in a hot oven on a rack for 45–60 minutes. Turn occasionally. Break skins to let the steam escape, add ½ tbs. butter, and a shake of paprika to each potato. Serve immediately.

Potato is the most useful vegetable for hash because it combines well with meat and other vegetables. Hash is an excellent way to use "left-overs."

THE BEAUTY AND UTILITY
OF "LEFT-OVERS"

So-called "left-overs" are a problem to every homemaker, and it is the wise cook who can either so merge them with other things that the identity is lost or make of them new dishes so palatable as to be desired rather than dreaded. With a little care and forethought, however, this can readily be done. The thrifty home manager exercises good judgment in the quantity of food she cooks. Many homemakers plan their dinners so that there will be something left for the next day's lunch. There are many nice ways of using vegetables and meats that have been cooked the day before, such as soups, casseroles, and salads that are easily prepared. These are equally pleasing in winter as in summer. By exercising care, no food need ever be wasted, and the food cupboard or refrigerator may always be kept free from scraps.

ECONOMICAL SOUPS. Soups are economical foods. They are wholesome and palatable and should form part of even the informal home dinner whenever possible. They are also excellent dishes for a luncheon or guest supper. If made carefully, they may be very tasty.

Economical Soup

1 qt. stock	1 bay leaf
1 onion	1 teaspoon salt
1 small carrot	1 sprig parsley
Leaves and root of celery stalk	Pinch of mace
2 cloves	Water to cover vegetables
2 peppercorns	

Chop the vegetables and cook them together with the herbs and seasoning in water sufficient to cover them. When done, add the stock and bring to a boil.

CASEROLE COOKERY. The importance of the casserole cookery can hardly be overemphasized in this day of high cost of living. All casserole foods are served in the dishes in which they are cooked, so there is no loss of heat in transference. The earthenware dishes are always attractive, whether encased in silver or not; the quaint artistic shapes make even a common article of food look interesting and attractive. There is also economy in pans and dishes, if that is a consideration.

SALADS. The salad may be regarded as an economic provision in the menu, for in no other way can so many left-overs be attractively presented upon the table. Many people limit the meaning of the word *salad* to the fresh green leaves, which are so refreshing and appetizing, but others apply the term to any kind of fruit, vegetable, fish, meat, or fowl to which a dressing has been added. Such salads may be the main dish in a meal. Many kinds of vegetables can be used as salads; nearly everyone uses them during the summer, but they are especially nice during the winter, when meals are apt to become rather monotonous. The thing of chief importance is to have everything crisp and cold. Greens should be carefully washed in cold water always. Dry by vigorous swinging in a wire basket or by pressing lightly between a clean folded towel or napkin.

Dandelion Salad

Gather young dandelion plants before they have flowered; cut off the roots; wash the greens thoroughly; boil in salted water about one hour, leaving the lid partly off. Drain and chop fine; season with salt, pepper, or vinegar and a liberal measure of butter.

SOUPS AND SAUCES

On a chilly winter day, nothing seems to make as good a beginning as a tasty hot soup. Besides being comforting and nutritious, soups allow the housekeeper's skill in thrift to shine when she uses all manner of left-overs in this delicious dish. The preparation of a sauce is of as much importance as the preparation of a dish itself and is frequently the supreme test of the cook's skill.

TYPES OF SOUPS. Soups, of which there is a countless variety, may be categorized as *clear* and *cream*. Clear soups are usually made from meat or chicken stock and are not thickened with flour or any other starchy material. White sauce combined with a vegetable, usually mashed or strained, makes cream soup. If you can make one kind of vegetable soup successfully, you should be able to make other kinds.

Stock: Stock is the basis of soups and may be made from meats or vegetables. *Bouillon* is the cleared stock made from beef. *Consommé* is the cleared stock made from two or three kinds of meat. Stock is used, in combination with other liquids, in soups, sauces, and gravies.

Basic Stock

2 lbs. meat, bone, and fat	½ bay leaf
2 quarts cold water	2½ tsp. salt
2 cloves	¼ tsp. celery seed
5 peppercorns	

Cut meat and fat into small pieces; cut bone into pieces. Cut off some of the fat and brown about one-third of the meat in it. Put all meat into a kettle, add seasoning and water; cover and allow to soak 1 hour. Then cook below the boiling temperature for 3 hours; strain through a coarse strainer. Set aside to cool. If fat has been allowed to solidify, skim from surface when stock is to be used. Tomatoes, carrots, turnips, and onion may be added.

Cream stock: This sauce recipe is used instead of stock as the foundation for many soups: Melt 1 tbs butter and add 1 tbs flour, being careful not to let it brown. Add 1 pint milk gradually, stirring constantly to prevent lumps; then add the seasoning (½ tsp salt, dash of red or black pepper). Refer to the table below for simple cream soup recipes.

Table 7. Cream-Soups Quick Guide

SOUP	PURÉE	VEGETABLE JUICE*	THIN WHITE SAUCE	ADDITIONAL INGREDIENT
Asparagus	1 cup	½ cup	1½ cups	—
Cauliflower	1 cup	—	2 cups	1 tbs. chopped parsley
Celery	1 cup	1 cup	1 cup	—
Corn	1 cup	—	2 cups	1 sliced onion
Mushroom	1 cup	1 cup	1 cup	—
Tomato	1 cup	—	2 cups	—

*Use the vegetable and the water in which it is cooked. Add salt and pepper.

SAUCES. The foundation for almost all of the common sauces is what the French call *roux*. This is butter and flour cooked together and thinned with milk, water, or other liquid. White sauce is made of milk thickened with flour. Under no circumstances should a sauce be thickened by adding a mixture of flour and water, as in this case the flour is seldom well cooked, or by adding flour alone, as this method is certain to cause lumps. The flour should be allowed to cook before the liquid is added.

If not served immediately, cover the sauce to prevent a crust from forming. Reheat when ready to serve.

PUTTING FOOD BY

Fresh fruit is usually more palatable and refreshing than cooked fruit, but it is not always obtainable. The importance of canning and preserving is therefore obvious. Canned goods of all sorts can be purchased, but they are usually inferior to the home-prepared foods.

Many homemakers refuse to can and preserve because they are scared. If proper care is taken, no harm can possibly befall the foods. The great secret of success in the canning of any food is absolute cleanliness. Fruit must be carefully picked and washed, and all stems removed, and only as much as can be cooked while it still retains its color and crispness should be prepared. Peaches, plums, and tomatoes may be readily skinned after a three-minute plunge in boiling water.

THE SCIENCE OF PRESERVING. Fruits and many other foods spoil because certain kinds of yeasts, molds, and bacteria grow on them and cause changes that make them unfit for us to eat. Therefore, it is necessary to kill all these organisms and to use jars that are free from germs and sealed so tightly that no germs can get in.

The first thing to do is to sterilize the jars (include the lids and rubbers, too). By *sterilizing* is meant the killing of all bacteria, yeasts, and molds. This is done by boiling the jars for about 20 minutes in a kettle of water. It is best first to wash the jars clean, rinse them, and put them on in a kettle of cold water; this tempers the jars as well as sterilizes them. To keep the jars from cracking, put a cloth in the bottom of the kettle and place the jars on their sides.

The beginning canner should start with high-acid foods, such as fruits, that can be safely canned using the open-kettle method. Low-acid foods, such as many vegetables, need higher temperatures, and often require the use of a pressure cooker.

KEEP IT CLEAN. Scrupulous cleanliness and eternal vigilance are the price of canning success. The kitchen should be freshly swept and dusted; the fruit should be carefully gone over and bruised or gnarled portions removed; and all jars and utensils should be thoroughly sterilized. Saucepans, spoons, jars, covers, straining bag, etc., should be put on the fire in cold water, heated gradually, and boiled for 10 or 15 minutes. The jars must be taken one at a time from the boiling water, and not removed until the moment each is to be filled.

Never use old rubbers or lids that are bent. Be sure that lids are boiled and rubbers dipped in boiling water just before using.

In canning fruits, there are several points to remember:
- No iron or tin utensils should be used, as the fruit acids attack these metals and so give a bad color and metallic taste to the food.
- All fruits should, if possible, be freshly picked, and it is better to have them underripe than overripe, as the fermentative stage follows closely upon the perfectly ripe stage.
- It is more satisfactory if fruits are heated gradually to the boiling point and then cooked the given time.

LABELING. Attractive labeling is just as necessary for jars in the home fruit cellar as for those offered for sale. It is always a good idea to write the contents when these may not be readily identified, and the date of canning as well.

OPEN-KETTLE METHOD. This method is one using an open kettle. The fruit is put into a kettle with a little liquid, boiled directly over the flame until tender, and then put into jars and sealed. It is most satisfactory for berries, jellies, jams, and fruit for sauce. The only vegetable to which it applies is the tomato.

The steps to be followed in canning by the open-kettle method:

1. Sterilize the jars, rubbers, and lids.
2. Prepare the fruits or vegetables by washing. Have them as clean as possible.
3. Have the required amount of liquid boiling hot, with the seasoning of sugar or salt as necessary.
4. Put the fruits or vegetables into the liquid and boil them until they are tender.
5. Put into the jars, seal quickly, and test for air bubbles by turning upside down.
6. Label the contents. Store in a cool, dark place when cold.

Canned Tomatoes
(Open-Kettle Method)

Select firm tomatoes and wash in cold water. Place in boiling water for 1 to 2 minutes, and then dip in cold water. Remove stem; peel and cut into pieces. Put into a kettle and bring slowly to the boiling point. Boil for 10 to 15 minutes. Fill sterilized jars to overflowing and seal at once.

JELLY. Jelly is made from sugar combined with the juice of fruits that contain acid and pectin. Ripe or overripe fruit does not contain as much pectin as underripe fruit. Some fruits like apples, quinces, grapes, and currants contain sufficient pectin to make jelly. Other fruits like peaches, pineapples, and strawberries do not contain enough pectin to jell. Try the recipe on the next page, using your favorite grape variety.

Grape Jelly

Wash the grapes and remove stems. Put into a kettle and cook slowly until grapes are soft. Mash as they cook, and drain through a coarse sieve. Allow the juice to drip through a double thickness of cheesecloth. Measure the juice, and add three fourths as much sugar. Boil until it measures 222°F. Turn into sterilized glasses. Cover with paraffin.

PICKLING. Another way of storing food for the winter is pickling, one of the oldest preservation methods. The term *pickling* is applied to the process of preserving food when either salt or vinegar is used. Pickled foods whet the appetite and help to make dishes—especially meat ones—more palatable. Below is the perfect recipe to use up your unripe tomatoes at the end of the season.

Green Tomato Pickle

1 peck tomatoes	2 tbs mustard
12 medium onions	2 tbs pepper berries
2 tbs salt	1 tbs whole allspice
3 pints vinegar	1 tbs whole cloves
3 c brown sugar	

Wash tomatoes and cut into slices. Peel and slice the onions. Add the salt and let drain overnight. Then add the sugar, vinegar, and spices (tied in a bag). Cook over medium heat just long enough to make them tender.

When fruit is preserved with a large amount of sugar (a pound of sugar to a pound of fruit), it does not need to be sealed in air-tight jars because bacteria do not readily form in the thick syrup. It is, however, best kept in small sealed jars since molds are likely to form.

THE HAPPY WORKING KITCHEN

When cooking, it is necessary to have the kitchen quiet, clean, and orderly. Good materials are essential, and only reliable recipes should be selected. The best maxim is: A place for everything, and everything in its place.

Before you begin:

✓ Collect all necessary material and utensils; also provide a utility plate on which to lay sticky knives, etc.

✓ Wash your hands with soap and water and scrub and clean your nails. If you handle anything not clean, wash your hands again.

✓ Have your hair neatly fastened back. Wear no jewelry.

✓ See that the oven will be ready for use at the time it is needed.

✓ Save dishes by measuring dry material first, then liquid, lastly fats.

Cooking tips and reminders:

- Leave the pan uncovered if you want to evaporate moisture.
- Cover baking foods if you wish to cook them without browning.
- Bake foods uncovered if you wish to brown them.
- A double boiler is great for cooking sauces as they are less likely to burn.
- Never taste with the mixing spoon.
- Clean your work as you go. Put egg and batter dishes to soak as soon as empty.
- Rinse containers and utensils after use.

Breaking a spoilt egg into your mixture will ruin the dish. Take care to use a separate receptacle.

The following are common terms used in recipes:

- *Baking* is cooking in a hot oven.
- *Boiling* is cooking in boiling water or other liquid.
- *Broiling* or *grilling* is cooking above coals, or directly over the fire.
- *Braising* and *fricasseeing* are combinations of sautéing and stewing.
- *Frying* is cooking in fat enough to cover the food completely.
- *Pan broiling* is cooking without fat in a hot frying pan or on a hot griddle.
- *Roasting* generally means cooking in an oven.
- *Steaming* is cooking over steam.
- *Stewing* is long, slow boiling in a small amount of water.

Manipulation of food:

- *To stir* is to put in motion.
- *To mix* is to blend.
- *To beat* is to force air into a mixture.
- *To knead* is to press and to fold alternately.
- *To cream* is to soften a substance by rubbing.
- *To pare* is to remove a skin by cutting.
- *To peel* is to remove a skin by tearing.
- *To fold* in egg whites or other substances is to combine them by making a vertical motion with a spoon to the bottom of the bowl, then sliding the spoon along the bottom and up the sides of the bowl, raising the spoon above the surface of the mixture and repeating the motion.
- *To dredge* is to sprinkle flour upon a surface.

The kitchen is the "heart of the house." As it is also the workshop, it must be arranged like one, with best regard for the work carried on there.

THE SERVING OF MEALS

Regardless of the manner in which a family lives, each one can help to make the meal a pleasant one. The appearance of the table and the food is of great importance.

There are three methods of serving meals:

1. *English*, used in ordinary family service. Foods are served at the table by the host and hostess and other members of the family. The served dishes may be passed from one person to another at the table. The hostess usually serves the soup, salad, and dessert; the host serves the meat and vegetables. This is the style of serving used in most American homes.

2. *Russian*, used for very formal meals. Each plate is served in the kitchen and placed in front of the guest; no serving-dishes are placed on the table. This form of service is not practical for the ordinary family, because it requires more work than the English service.

3. *Combination*, used for informal meals. This is a combination of the two other styles. For example, the soup or salad is served in the kitchen, and the meat and vegetables are served at the table.

Removing and replacing a plate. With a clean plate in the right hand, go to the left side of the person being served. Remove the soiled plate with the left hand and put in its place a clean plate.

Serving tips:

- Place as many dishes and as much food as possible on the table before the family is seated. Bread, butter, salt, pepper, sugar, cream, water, and all necessary dishes should be on the table.

- Make as few trips as possible between the dining room and kitchen, especially when the meal is being served.

- When serving a meal, never go empty-handed on the trips between kitchen and dining room. If you carry soiled dishes from the dining room to the kitchen, return with something to complete the meal.

- When refilling water glasses, do not lift the glass from the table. Have a clean napkin in the left hand to catch drops that may drip from the pitcher after pouring.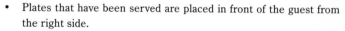

- Serving dishes from which the guest is to serve himself must be passed to the left of the guest.

- Plates that have been served are placed in front of the guest from the right side.

- When removing dishes between the courses, use the following order: remove the used dishes, then the dishes containing food, next the clean dishes and silver that will not be needed further, then the crumbs from the cloth. A table never looks attractive when dirty dishes from one course remain during the next course, and even at the most informal meals it is better to remove dishes between courses.

 Regardless of how well food is cooked, if it is brought to the table hurriedly or carelessly, the meal cannot be enjoyed thoroughly.

THE ELEGANT TABLE

Artistic table appointments give pleasure and satisfaction to every member of the family. At very little expense, almost any homemaker can have dishes and glassware that are delightful in color and design.

Everything required for setting the table should be stored in the most convenient place in order not to waste time or effort in doing this frequently performed task. Find how long it takes to lay the table in your home and try to reduce the time by rearranging the supply of linen, china, glassware, and silverware, and by using a tray to save steps.

PLACING THE DISHES AT EACH COVER. A *cover* is the space and utensils used by one person at a meal. The arrangement of the utensils of the cover is very similar for breakfast, lunch, or dinner (see illustrations). For dinner, the napkins, plates, knives, and forks are usually larger than for other meals. A wide display of silver is not in good taste.

A Breakfast Cover

A Lunch Cover

A Dinner Cover

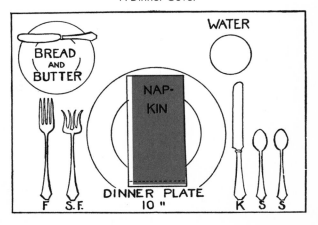

A GRACEFUL TABLE MANNER

Certain rules for table behavior or manners have been adopted because they make the eating of the meal easier and more graceful, and the serving of it more convenient. Whether the family is alone or entertaining, be sure to set the table correctly and carefully. Practice the same table manners every day, for there is no such thing as "company manners." Below are a few reminders of polite utensil use.

Proper Placement and Use of Utensils

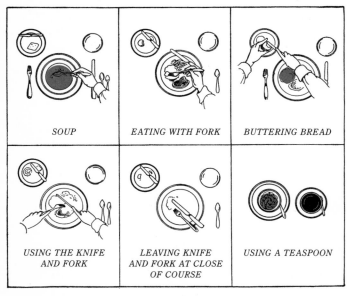

SOUP	*EATING WITH FORK*	*BUTTERING BREAD*
USING THE KNIFE AND FORK	*LEAVING KNIFE AND FORK AT CLOSE OF COURSE*	*USING A TEASPOON*

The following are important rules that should be observed always when at the dining table:

- Never go to the table unless hands are clean.
- No one should be seated at the table until the hostess takes her seat, nor should anyone start to eat until the hostess gives the signal.
- Always sit erect in the chair while eating. Keep the arms and elbows off the table.
- Never eat hurriedly.
- Do not talk when the mouth is full of food.
- Ask politely for dishes to be passed, rather than reaching across the table for them.
- Do not talk about disagreeable things during the meal.
- Always come to the table promptly. If unavoidably delayed, or if it is necessary to leave the table before the meal is finished, try not to disturb the others, but quietly say to the hostess, "May I be excused?"
- The napkin should be laid across the lap without being entirely opened out. Never stick the corner inside the collar. Use the corner of the napkin to wipe the lips when necessary. If the napkin is to be used again, fold it neatly before leaving the table.
- Always use the napkin before drinking from a glass.
- The knife should be held in the right hand and should be used for cutting only, excepting the individual butter knife, which is used for cutting and spreading butter.
- The fork is held in the left hand when cutting, and it is permissible to keep the fork in the left hand when eating.

 No matter how educated or pleasing in character one may be, the impression made upon others is not good if one's manners are poor.

CARVING TECHNIQUES

The meat dish is often the main attraction of the meal, therefore careful carving is necessary in order to present the meat at its best. The skilled homekeeper knows how to wield a sharp knife and make short work of serving up a roast or whole bird.

Carving turkey:
1. *First remove a leg.* Cut through the skin and meat covering the joint next to the body. Then break the joint by grasping the end of the leg with the fingers and pulling away from the body. Now separate the loosened leg into drumstick and second joint by cutting through the joint uniting the two parts.
2. *Remove a wing.* Separate the joint next to the body in the same way as the leg joint.
3. *Slice the breast.* Stick the fork into the breast near the highest point of the breast bone; then cut into thin slices.

1. REMOVE A LEG.

2. REMOVE A WING.

3. SLICE THE BREAST.

Carving meat:

1. In carving steak containing bone, first cut out the bone, then cut into pieces.

2. First cut the top string of a roiled roast, then slice thinly across grain of meat. When necessary, cut the other strings.

3. To carve a standing roast, turn the meat so the rib bones point to you. Slice thinly toward bone. When several slices are cut, loosen them by cutting along the edge of bone with the point of the knife.

4. Starting at the larger end of a whole ham, cut it into thin slices. Loosen the slices from the bone as directed in number 3.

5. To carve a pot roast, separate a portion of the meat from the bones. Then cut the loosened piece *across the grain* into slices ¼- to ½-inch thick. Serve two or three slices to each person.

1. STEAK   *2. ROILED ROAST*

3. STANDING ROAST   *4. HAM*

5. POT ROAST

MEASURING WITH CARE

To obtain good results in cooking, it is necessary to have accurate measurements. Good cooking is not the result of good luck but of careful work. For accurate measurements, use the standard-size measuring cup, tablespoon, and teaspoon, and be sure measurements are level. Flour and confectioner's sugar should be sifted before measuring and must not be tapped or packed in the cup. Measure dry materials first, liquids second, and fats last to avoid soiling unnecessary dishes.

Techniques for measuring:

- For a spoonful, dip the spoon into the material, lift it, and level off true with a spatula or knife.
- For a cupful, fill the cup with the aid of a spoon, and level off with a spatula or knife (see illustration, below).
- In measuring dry material, such as flour, baking powder, baking soda, powdered sugar, or spices, sift or shake up lightly before measuring and do not dip cup into the material, which packs it, but fill with a spoon.
- To measure butter or lard, pack solidly into cup with a spoon.
- A *heaping* teaspoon or cup means all it will hold.
- A *scant* teaspoon or cup is a little less than level measure.

Efficient measuring. Spoon dry material into a cup, then leaven with a knife. Although part of a cupful can be measured in a measuring cup, fractional-cup measuring can be done more efficiently by using a set of measuring cups.

Common culinary abbreviations:

- tbs. or T. stands for tablespoon
- tsp. stands for teaspoon
- oz. stands for ounce
- lb. stands for pound
- h. stands for hour

- qt. stands for quart
- pt. stands for pint
- spk. stands for speck
- c. stands for cup
- m. stands for minute

MEASUREMENTS AND THEIR EQUIVALENTS. When following recipes, it is often necessary to convert one type of measurement into the equivalent of another measure. For example, a recipe calls for a pint of material, and you have a measuring cup but no pint measure. The following chart should help.

Equivalents

4 c.	1 qt.	2 c. rice	1 lb.
2 c.	1 pt.	4 c. flour	1 lb.
16 tbs.	1 c.	4 c. coffee unground	1 lb.
8 tbs.	½ c.	6 c. tea.	1 lb.
4 tbs.	¼ c.	3½ c. cocoa	1 lb.
3 tsp.	1 tbs.	8–10 eggs	1 lb.
60 drops.	1 tsp.	1 sq. chocolate	1 oz.
2 c. butter	1 lb.	1 pk. (40 potatoes)	15 lbs.
2 c. fat	1 lb.	1 large lemon	¼ c. juice
2 c. gran. sugar.	1 lb.	1 large orange	½ c. juice

Wooden spoons are best for cooking. It is a good plan to nail a piece of leather in some convenient place, with spaces between every nail, rather loose, to admit the handle of the spoon; they may be thus kept out of the way.

HOME-BAKED BREAD

It may be true that one cannot live by bread alone, but this delicious staple surely holds an important place in the diet. And since homemade bread is infinitely more palatable and more nutritious than baker's bread, it is worthwhile to spend some time and effort in its preparation.

The three essentials in bread-making are flour, yeast, and liquid. Yeast is a microscopic plant and needs light, heat, and moisture to grow; it grows best in a temperature of about 86°F. Bread should therefore be set to rise in a warm place, free from drafts; but too great heat must be avoided. Above 90°F, and the conditions are favorable for the growth of lactic acid bacteria, and the bread "sours." Bread must be covered while rising to prevent a crust from forming on the top of the dough.

There are many different types of bread due to different materials and ways of working. Once you've mastered the art of making plain white bread (as in the recipe, right), and understand the reasons for doing certain things (like kneading and rising), it's easy to make any kind you wish.

KNEADING TIPS. Bread dough must be kneaded or stirred well. Kneading or stirring is necessary not only to mix the ingredients, but also to form gluten from the proteins of the flour and to distribute the carbon dioxide uniformly through the dough. Review the illustration below for proper technique.

Kneading bread. Flour your fingers and palms. Place them on the dough. Quickly and lightly press down with the palms. Turn the dough (quarter turn). Press again. Repeat, kneading the dough for at least 5 minutes or until it is smooth and elastic.

Qualities of a good loaf of white bread:

✓ Crust should be smooth, golden brown, without cracks or bulges.

✓ The inside should be creamy white in color with fine holes evenly distributed, smooth and moist in texture, and light in weight.

✓ The flavor should be sweet and nutlike.

Loaf Bread
(Two loaves)

2 tbs. sugar	1 tbs. fat
1 pt. boiling water or scalded milk	1 or 2 cakes compressed yeast
2 tsp. salt	Flour, about 8 c.

1. Into a mixing bowl, put the sugar, salt, fat, and water or milk. Cool until lukewarm. When lukewarm, crumble the yeast into the water mixture and mix.

2. Sift 1 c. of flour into the yeast mixture. Mix well; add as much more sifted flour as you can work with.

3. Turn the dough onto a slightly floured board. Knead.

4. Put the dough into a greased mixing bowl. Cover tightly and put in a warm (not hot) place. When doubled in bulk, turn out on a slightly floured mixing board. Knead a second time.

5. Cut the dough in two. Shape each part into a loaf. Place each in a greased pan or oven-glass dish. Put the pans in a warm (not hot) place. Cover with a clean towel and let rise.

6. When the loaves are at least twice their original size, bake at 375°F for 1 hour, until sufficiently baked.

7. Place the loaves on a cake cooler. To soften crust, rub butter over it.

Two risings are sufficient for bread if the ingredients have been well mixed. Dough permitted to rise until too light will be full of holes; bread baked before it is sufficiently light will be heavy.

BAKING THE PERFECT CAKE

Every good cook prides herself upon the quality of her products in the particular field of cake-making. Much depends upon the way she does her work, for a cake may be light, spongy, and fairly digestible or it may be heavy, soggy, and incapable of digestion even by the most healthy person. The baking is especially important, because even good cake poorly baked is unfit to eat.

CAKE REQUIREMENTS. Besides using accurate measurements, good materials are needed for successful cake baking. If a cake contains no ingredients of pronounced flavor, such as spices, chocolate, or molasses, the sugar and shortening are the chief flavoring materials. For these, use flavorsome fats, such as butter or margarine. Eggs are another important cake ingredient. Choose only the freshest.

Cake-making essentials:
- Pastry or cake flour produces a daintier cake than all-purpose or bread flour.
- Use only the best ingredients.
- Use accurate measures.
- Never grease pans for cakes made *without* butter. Do grease pans for cakes made *with* butter.
- The position of the pans in the oven and correct oven temperature are important factors.

Stagger pans. To avoid interference with circulation of air, stagger pans when placing more than one in the oven.

CAKE FAILURES. Cakes are sometimes disappointing, They may turn out more like bread than cake. They may be coarse in grain, they may fall, they may crack across the top; they may have a host of other faults. The following causes are responsible for such defects. Observe that many of the faults may be due to careless measuring.

Causes of Cake Failures

CAUSES	DEFECTS
Too much sugar	Coarse grain; hard, grainy crust
Too little sugar	Tough, heavy, flavor not good
Too much shortening	Crumbly, too compact, may fall
Too little shortening	Dry, tough, tasteless
Too much flour or too little liquid	Cracked crust; heavy crumb
Too much baking powder	Coarse grain, flavor off
Too little flour or too much liquid	Too compact, may fall, run over
Too little baking powder	Heavy, under size, tough
Too much beating	Tough, heavy, dry, under size
Too little beating	Coarse crumb
Too little creaming of fat and sugar	Coarse grain; sugar-spotted crust
Too high temperature	Hard, thick, dark, cracked crust
Too low temperature	Coarse, dry crumb; under size

Cake is done when it shrinks from the sides of the pan. Press the top of the cake with the finger; if it springs back into place, it is done.

CLASSES OF CAKES. Whether a cake batter contains shortening determines the class to which it belongs. Cakes are commonly divided into two classes—cakes *with* and *without* butter. Whatever shortening is used, it must be mixed thoroughly with the other ingredients. The shortening should first be creamed (made soft and pliable with a spoon) and then blended thoroughly with sugar.

Plain Cake

2¼ c. sifted cake flour *(a)*	½ c. butter or shortening
2 tsp. baking powder	1 c. sugar
¼ tsp. salt	1 tsp. vanilla
2 eggs, separated	¾ c. milk

1. Measure and sift dry ingredients. Put the fat in a mixing bowl. If hard, let stand until pliable. With a wooden spoon, work fat until soft. Add ¾ c. sugar gradually, creaming as the sugar is added *(b)*.
2. After separating the eggs, let them stand until they are room temperature. Beat the whites until stiff but not dry. Add ¼ c. sugar. Beat enough to mix. With the same beater, beat the egg yolks. Add yolks and vanilla to the sugar mixture.
3. Sift a portion of the dry ingredients (about ¼) into the sugar mixture. Quickly mix. Continue adding and mixing the dry and moist ingredients, ending with dry. Stir only until the batter is smooth *(c)*. Cut and fold the beaten egg whites into batter as in making omelet. Line the bottom of two 8-inch layer cake pans or one loafcake pan with waxed paper. Grease edges of pan and pour in batter. Bake layers at 375°F 30 to 35 minutes, loaf at 350°F 40 to 60 minutes.
4. Take pans from oven and let stand 2 minutes on a cake cooler. Remove cakes and place the layers right side up on cooler until cold.

---

a. Or use 2 cups all-purpose flour.

b. Reserve ¼ cup sugar to mix with beaten egg whites.

c. Mix dry and moist ingredients quickly. Do not overstir, lest a tough undersize cake results.

Table 8. Butter Cake Variations

KIND OF CAKE	CAKE FLOUR SIFTED (a)	BAKING POWDER	BAKING SODA	SALT	FAT	SUGAR	EGGS	FLAVORINGS	LIQUID	CHOCOLATE
	c.	tsp.	tsp.	tsp.	c.	c.	No.	tsp.	c.	Oz.
Plain	2¼	2	—	¼	¼	1	1 or 2	1 vanilla	1 milk	—
Chocolate	2¼	2	¼	¼	¼	1¼	3	1 vanilla	1 milk	2
Spice	2¼	1½	½	¼	¼	1 brown	1 or 2	1 cinnamon nutmeg ¼ cloves	1 sour milk	—
Rich	2¼	2	—	½	½	1½	3	1½ vanilla	1 milk	—
White	2½	2	—	½	½	1½	4 whites only	1 vanilla ½ almond	1 water	—

a. If all-purpose is used, decrease to 2 cups.

QUICK BREADS

Quick breads seem to find favor in nearly every family. They offer variety in the diet and in some form are enjoyed by most people. They are so easily made that they appear frequently on the breakfast or luncheon table.

Quick breads are those that are baked immediately after mixing, as contrasted with the yeast breads, which must be allowed time to rise. Muffins are quick breads, too. Quick breads are made light or porous with baking powder, or with baking soda if sour milk is one of the ingredients. Baking powder and baking soda are quick-acting leavening agents. By contrast, yeast, the leavening agent of "raised bread," acts more slowly. Try the recipes on these pages to add a delightful and delicious quick bread to your meal.

Plain Muffins

2 c. all-purpose sifted flour	½ tsp. salt
2 or 4 tsp. baking powder	2 to 4 tbs. sugar
1 egg	4 tbs. butter or other fat
1 c. milk	

1. Sift some flour, then measure it, preferably in a pint measure. Add the measured baking powder and salt to the flour.
2. Beat the egg in a mixing bowl. Add the milk and sugar.
3. Measure and melt shortening. Add it to the egg mixture. Mix.
4. Sift the dry ingredients into the egg mixture. Quickly mix the ingredients with not more than 25 strokes of the spoon.
5. Fill each muffin cup about ¾ full. Bake at 400°F for 25 min.

The preparation of all kinds of food demands a clean worker, and immaculate hands are necessary when they are to come in such close contact with food, as is necessary when handling dough in the making of bread or biscuit.

Table 9. Other Kinds of Muffins and Cinnamon Bread
Follow directions for mixing plain muffins (opposite page).

KIND	FLOUR OR MEAL	BAKING POWDER	SUGAR	SALT	EGGS	LIQUID	FAT	OTHER INGREDIENTS
Corn meal	1 c. pastry or all-purpose flour (a) 2 tbs. corn meal (b)	3 tsp.	2 to 4 tbs.	1 tsp.	1	1 c. milk	4 tbs.	
Whole or entire wheat	1 c. pastry or all-purpose flour (a) 1 c. whole wheat (b)	3 tsp.	2 to 4 tbs.	½ tsp.	1	1 c. milk	4 tbs.	½ c. chopped nuts
Date or raisin or apricot	2 c. pastry or all-purpose flour (d)	3 tsp.	2 to 4 tbs.	½ tsp.	1	1 c. milk (c)	4 tbs.	¾ c. stoned dates or apricots (cut into pieces with wet scissors) or raisins
Orange	2 c. pastry or all-purpose flour (d)	3 tsp.	4 tbs.	½ tsp.	1	¾ c. milk; ¼ c. orange juice	4 tbs.	1 tsp. grated orange rind
Blueberry or cranberry	2 c. pastry or all-purpose flour (d)	2 tsp.	½ c.	½ tsp.	1	½ c. milk	5 tbs.	1 c. blueberries or cranberries (e)
Cinnamon bread (f)	2 c. pastry or all-purpose flour (d)	3 tsp.	½ c. to ¾ c.	½ tsp.	1	1 c. milk	4 tbs.	

a. If cake flour is substituted, use 1 c. plus 2 tbs; *b.* Do not put meal or coarse flours through a sifter; *c.* Heat the milk. Add washed fruit. Let stand until cool; *d.* If cake flour is substituted, use 2¼ c; *e.* Wash fruit before mixing. Drain well. Mix egg, milk, sugar, and melted fat. Sift in other dry ingredients, then add berries and mix; *f.* Pour into a shallow square pan, 9 x 9 inches. Cover with the following topping: 2 tbs. sugar, ½ tsp. powdered cinnamon.

MAKING CANDY

Making candy can be a lot of fun, but it can also be very difficult. It is advisable to use a candy thermometer. The base of most candies is a syrup and milk or water. Among the changes that take place when the syrup cooks are *(a)* the liquid evaporates, making the syrup heavier or thicker, and *(b)* the syrup becomes hotter, or its temperature rises. The temperature of a syrup is an indication of its thickness. Try your hand at candymaking with the recipes on the next page.

THERMOMETER ACCURACY. When using a candy thermometer, immerse the bulb in the syrup, but do not let it touch the bottom or sides of the pan. When a candy thermometer is immersed in boiling water, it should read 212°F/100°C. The accuracy of your thermometer can be tested by trying it in boiling water. If you do not have a thermometer, use the water test, dropping only a few drops of syrup into a cup of ice water. This test is fairly satisfactory for those who have used it repeatedly.

Thermometer and Cold-Water Test for Candy

CANDY	TEMPERATURE	COLD-WATER TEST
Fudge, panocha, fondant	234°–240°	Soft ball (forms when shaped with fingers)
Caramels	246°–250°	Firm ball
Taffy to be pulled . . . Molasses . . . White	265° 268°	Hard (not brittle) ball
Popcorn balls and butterscotch	270°–290°	Soft crack (slightly brittle)
Lollipops and other clear brittle candies	300°–310°	Hard crack (very brittle, but not scorched)

Butter Taffy

2 c. brown sugar
¼ c. butter
¼ tsp. salt

1 tbs. vinegar or juice of ½ lemon
¼ c. water

Mix all the ingredients together in a smooth saucepan. Cook slowly, stirring until the sugar dissolves. Sir occasionally to prevent burning and cook until the syrup is brittle when tested in cold water (275°F). Pour into a buttered pan and mark into squares while warm.

Peanut Brittle

1 qt. roasted peanuts
1 lb. granulated sugar

Shell the peanuts; remove the skins and roll them or run them through the meat chopper. Melt the sugar; add the peanuts; mix and turn out on a greased marble slab or large greased tin. Roll quickly with an ordinary rolling pin that has been well greased; cut into squares and break apart.

Popcorn Balls

3 quarts popped corn
1 c. sugar
1 c. brown sugar
½ c. water

½ c. corn syrup
1 tbs. butter
1 teaspoon salt

Separate the popped kernels from the unpopped ones. Mix all other ingredients except butter in a saucepan. Cook to 242°F, or until the candy becomes slightly brittle when dropped into cold water. Add the butter. Stir slightly to mix. Slowly pour the syrup over the popped corn, stirring to mix. Shape the corn into balls.

Homemade candy made with molasses, milk, butter, or nuts may not be as attractive as some of the bought candies, but the food value is much greater.

"Care of clothing is a duty. It is necessary to be particular about personal appearance at all times, for being appropriately dressed helps one in achieving success in life."

Care
of Clothing
and Textiles

Simplicity in dress and in living are fine mottoes. Happiness really does not depend on luxurious living, and it is certainly unwise and in bad form to live or dress extravagantly at any time. Garments that are overtrimmed or poor in construction, line, and color are not worth buying.

Care of clothing is a duty. It is necessary to be particular about personal appearance at all times, for being appropriately dressed helps one in achieving success in life. Cleanliness and neatness are great helpers, and one is not well dressed unless one thinks about these things. Clothing that is clean, in repair, in good taste, and appropriate is a necessary part of a well-groomed appearance. To be good-looking, one must be careful about the selection, care, and manner of wearing all types of clothing.

THE PURCHASE OF CLOTHING AND SHOES

Clothing and shoes, like food, must be considered in relation to health and efficiency. Proper clothing is one of the means of promoting health. Clothing must give proper ventilation to the skin. Healthful clothing should be of such materials that it not only aids in maintaining the right temperature but also takes care of the perspiration so that the skin is cooled rapidly in warm weather and not too rapidly in cool weather.

THOUGHTFUL SELECTION. Limited income does not necessarily imply unbecoming clothes, so select garments that are pleasing to the eye, becoming to the wearer, and harmonious in tone. In buying ready-made garments, there are many things to consider:

- Is the garment made under sanitary conditions? Many garments are made in sweatshops that are dirty, poorly aired, and in every way an unfit place for women and girls to work.
- Know what your needs are before you go to the store.
- Is the material of good quality and suitable for the garment?
- Is the garment well made, so that the seams will hold and the trimmings not pull apart? Coarse or crooked stitching spoils the appearance of a garment.
- Select comfortable, hygienic, and attractive garments.
- A few garments of good quality are a much better investment than many cheap ones.
- Beware of bargain sales unless you are an experienced shopper.
- Conservative styles are in better taste than extreme styles.

When buying a garment, one must also consider the laundering and wearing qualities. Remember: A garment with elaborate trims will cost more in time and energy to clean.

BEING WELL SHOD. It pays to buy shoes of good quality. Such shoes are not only made of more durable material but cut and made more carefully. Accurate workmanship will make them feel better. Moreover, they will look well for a longer time because they will keep their shape.

If one must economize on shoes, it is better to pay less for shoes for dress or party wear.

It is also essential that shoes fit correctly. Shoes that are put on shoe trees as soon as they are removed will keep their shape much longer. Having heels and toes repaired before the damage has gone too far is thrifty. The following suggestions may help when buying shoes.

Length of shoe: Observe the length of your shoe with reference to the end of your toe while you are sitting and standing.

Width of shoe and shape of toe: A shoe should be broad enough to allow the toes to spread when the wearer is standing or walking. The heel should be broad enough to support the body.

Height of heel: The heel should be low or medium in height. High heels are not suitable for street wear. If you must wear extreme shoes, wear them only for dress or dancing.

Size of heel: The heel should be broad and fit snugly.

Position of the ball of the foot: The ball of the foot should rest on the widest part of the sole. When trying shoes, notice whether the joint of the big toe is just above the widest part of the shoe's sole.

Points to check when buying shoes.
A. Height of heel—¾ inch to 1½ inches is proper for everyday wear.
B. Rigid shank recommended.
C. Large toe joint over widest part of sole.
D. Thick soles recommended for walking.

A LESSON IN THE PRINCIPLES OF DESIGN

In order to be well-dressed, we must know good design and how to secure it. A good design shows not only an orderly arrangement but also beauty in the finished product.

A beautiful dress is planned by the same principles that an artist uses in painting beautiful pictures or an interior decorator in furnishing a home. To know how to select attractive garments that are pleasing in design and line requires that you learn about these principles of design: balance, emphasis, rhythm, and proportion, which produce unity and harmony.

BALANCE. The success of every design depends in a measure upon correct balance, which gives a feeling of rest. This restful effect is obtained by grouping shapes and colors around a center in such a way that there will be equal attractions on each side.

EMPHASIS. Emphasis is really secured through subordination, which requires only one center of interest in the design and that all else shall be subordinated to it.

RHYTHM. Rhythm, or related movement, which is produced by repetition, causes an object to appear as a whole and not disconnected. The eye easily follows from one part to another, creating a feeling of beauty. Rhythm may be obtained in any ensemble by flowing rhythm, an easily connected or continuous curved line; marching rhythm, a regular repetition; and progressive rhythm, or gradation.

PROPORTION. Every time two or more objects are placed together, either good or bad space division, or proportion, is established. Space relations are considered good when it is somewhat difficult to detect the divisions, but monotonous when spaces are equal.

The Greek Law of Proportion: Some people have an instinct for good proportion, but those who have to train themselves should adopt the "Greek Law of Proportion," or ratios of two to three, three to five, four to seven, and five to eight. To illustrate this law of proportion in a garment, if we wished to place a jacket on a dress we would first construct an oblong equal in dimension to the front area of the dress, then divide the oblong into halves and then into thirds. The jacket length would be about halfway between the one-half and the two-thirds division.

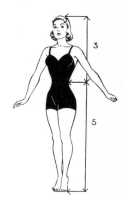

UNITY AND HARMONY. An object that has unity has "oneness," or completeness. Nothing can be taken away and nothing needs to be added. This is brought about through harmony, or a pleasing relation to all of the parts. When making or buying a dress, consider the entire garment to determine if all the parts go together.

Harmony in shape. The parts of the one blouse are unrelated in shape. In the other, the scallops, round buttons, and belt buckle harmonize in shape.

CARE AND STORAGE

The length of time a garment may be worn can be increased by proper care. Good care of clothing requires that some thought and energy shall be used every day, but since a well-cared-for garment wears longer and always looks better, the effort is worthwhile.

Clothing is well cared for when:
- ✓ All spots and stains have been removed.
- ✓ It has had the proper brushing, pressing, and airing.
- ✓ The shoes are polished and clean.
- ✓ All rips, tears, worn places, and holes have been repaired.
- ✓ It is laundered or cleaned.
- ✓ The stockings are mended.
- ✓ The accessories are clean and ready to wear.
- ✓ It is properly hung in the closet.
- ✓ The drawers are neat and in order.

AVOIDING WRINKLES AND SPOTS. The time spent in pressing clothes may be lost if they are left overnight in a heap on the floor or carelessly thrown across a chair. After removing clothing, place the garment at once on a hanger. If your closet is tightly closed, it is well not to place the item there immediately. If possible, hang it where it will air. Clothes that have been dry cleaned should be hung to dry in an airy place until the odor that clings to them has disappeared.

It is easier to prevent clothes from spotting than it is to remove the spots. When working in the kitchen or around the house, protect your clothes with an apron. If you do spot a spot, try the cleaning method described below.

Spot removal: Remove a spot from a garment as soon as possible after it appears. Place a folded towel or clean cloth underneath the spotted part of the garment. With a clean cloth, apply the cleaning fluid, rubbing lightly along lengthwise or crosswise thread of the garment from outside to center. If the spot has not disappeared, apply more cleaning fluid, but do not use too much at a time.

PROTECTING FROM DUST. Even if your clothes are hung in a tightly closed closet, some dust will collect on them. It pays to cover clothes, especially those that are worn only occasionally. All sorts of bags and covers designed to protect clothes may be made or purchased. Dust that collects on clothes worn on the street should, of course, be removed by brushing.

MAKING YOUR CLOTHES CLOSET EFFICIENT. An efficient clothes closet has hat and shoe racks, transparent hat boxes, and garment bags. If you need more storage space and do not have a pole in your closet, arrange to put one up. The handle of a discarded broom or mop will often do very well.

Shoes on the floor of a bedroom or clothes closet make the rooms untidy and make cleaning difficult. A shoes bag or rack on the inside of a closet door is a convenient device for storing shoes.

If space is an issue, pack away out-of-season clothes, sealing the container tightly to avoid moth damage. The essential thing is that the garments are well aired, brushed, and thoroughly cleansed before being put away. Woolens, furs, and dresses should be brushed and all spots removed. In this way, no good material is wasted.

Spots on clothing look careless and spoil a neat appearance. Being careful with one's clothes every day helps to save much time in cleaning and repairing.

CAREFUL LAUNDERING

Laundering is interesting and profitable work if well done. Cleanliness adds to our comfort, but we all know that it costs time, money, and energy. Laundering, if properly done, conserves clothing, and one will think of this if one is thrifty.

WASH-DAY BASICS. There should be a definite place for leaving all soiled clothing and linens to await wash day. Before items are washed, each article should be inspected for spots and needed repairs.

Tears that may become worse in laundering and broken stitches should be mended before they are laundered. Whites should be washed in hot water; and colors in warm. Delicates that can go in the machine should be washed in cold water.

One of the most important of the laundry processes is the rinsing. Clothing must be thoroughly rinsed to remove all of the soap and washing powder. The rinsing should be warm (except in the case of delicates) in order that the soap and remaining dirt can be removed. Other points to bear in mind are the following:

Strong soap — Hardens and shrinks woolens. Yellows white silks. Removes color in colored materials.

Rubbing — Wears all fabrics. Hardens woolens. Gives silk a rough and wavy look. Injures color.

Sunlight — Bleaches and whitens white cotton and linen. Hardens and shrinks woolens. Yellows white silks and woolens. Fades colors.

Temperature — Sudden changes harden and shrink woolens. Anything hotter than lukewarm injures silk and may change or remove color from any fabric.

SPECIAL INSTRUCTIONS FOR WOOL. Because woolen materials shrink greatly if not laundered properly, great care should be used in handling them. Because a sweater is made of wool and is knitted, it may shrink excessively or stretch out of shape. The method of laundering and temperature of water make a great deal of difference in the shrinkage of wool garments. Follow these steps for shrink-free success.

1. Use lukewarm water and make a rich suds of any neutral soap.
2. Wash only one piece at a time.
3. Do not soak, boil, or rub woolen materials.
4. Punch and knead the garment in the suds until it is clean.
5. If one soapy washing is not enough, use a second one.
6. Wring out the soapy water by squeezing.
7. Rinse the garment thoroughly through two or three waters of the same lukewarm temperature.
8. Squeeze the water out and shake the garment.
9. Hang in a warm, shady place and let dry thoroughly. While drying, the garment should be shaped by pulling and stretching. When partly dry, the garment should be turned.
10. Lay a damp cloth over the garment and press with a hot iron.

LAUNDRY ETIQUETTE. It is usually more convenient to do your hand washing in the bathroom than in the laundry or kitchen. When you decide to do your washing in the bathroom, be sure you are not inconveniencing someone else by occupying it for too long a time; and do not infringe on the rights and comfort of other members of the family by hanging your laundered garments on their towel bars. Rather, hang the laundered clothes in the laundry room or out of doors.

FRESH-SMELLING UNDERGARMENTS. Every homemaker should know how to launder undergarments to make them last as long as possible, keep their color, and look their best. We can wear our underclothes sometimes without ironing if they have been washed clean.

All fine and delicate fabrics require special care. If properly handled in washing, they will retain their natural beauty and wearing quality. White rayon does not become yellowed with laundering, as white silk does. Follow these steps for washing dainty delicates.

1. Use lukewarm water. Make a rich suds of any good soap.
2. Squeeze or work the garment in the suds. Handle quickly. Do not rub or twist hard. Repeat the suds bath if necessary to thoroughly cleanse the garment.
3. Rinse thoroughly through several waters of lukewarm temperature.
4. Squeeze the water from the garment.
5. Dry the garment by either: *(a)* wrapping it in a cloth and letting it lie a while, *(b)* hanging it in a shady place.

To wash hosiery, follow the directions above, squeezing the water by wrapping in a towel. Allow to drip-dry.

DRYING. To some it might seem that the laundry work is practically done when clothes are ready to be hung on the line. But oversight in the drying might make necessary the rewashing of articles. One of the chief virtues of proper drying of clothes is the effect that sun and air have on them. When clothes are hung on the line quite wet, almost dripping in fact, the combined action of sun and air is one of the best bleaches known. It is because of this that white clothes should be hung, when possible, out of doors, and that colored clothes should be hung in the shade or indoors.

To save time in the sorting of articles for ironing, hang all garments of a kind together. Then, to have the clothes dry in the best possible condition, keep in mind the following general directions:

- Be sure that clothes line and pins are perfectly clean.
- Shake things out well.
- Hang large pieces, such as sheets and tablecloths, on a straight thread of the material, one-fourth or one-half of each over the line, and fasten with four or five clothes pins.
- Fold flat pieces as they are taken off the line, as then they will be easier to iron.
- A garment will dry more quickly if hung by the hem.

Methods of Stain Removal

STAIN	USE
Acid	Lukewarm water.
Blood	Cold water. Soak, then wash in warm suds.
Chocolate	Cold water.
Cocoa	Cold water.
Coffee	Lukewarm water.
Egg	Lukewarm water.
Fruit	Boiling water.
Grass	Rub with cold water.
Grease	Lukewarm water.
Ink	Cold water.
Iron rust	Lemon juice.
Paint	Turpentine.
Punch	Boiling water.
Tea	Lukewarm water.

IRONING. Ironing is really an art. A homemaker who keeps her family's linens and clothes in good condition should plan to do some ironing at least once a week. Some like to set aside a part of Saturday morning.

Clothing irons best when it is carefully sprinkled so that all parts are uniformly moist. If material is plain and smooth, its ironing may be finished on the right side. Pieces that have straight edges, such as towels and napkins, should be pulled straight before ironing. Corded or embroidered materials or lace should be ironed only on the wrong side. Always iron in the direction of lengthwise or crosswise threads.

Special care should be taken when ironing a blouse, especially if it has frilly decorative treatments or trimmings. Follow these steps for a smartly pressed look.

1. Iron the sleeves of the blouse first, then the front and back.
2. Iron tucks lengthwise, first stretching them into shape.
3. Iron ruffles first along the edge; then point the nose of the iron into the gathered portion.
4. Don't forget the placket and around the buttons!

Suggestions for ironing flat pieces: Iron cotton and linens on the right side except where there is embroidery work, beading, buttons, or other fasteners. Such a surface should be laid on a thick, soft towel or blanket so that the embroidery work or fasteners will be pressed down into the padded surface, and then ironed on the wrong side.

FOLDING CLOTHES. If this step is treated as an important one, worthy of systematizing, it can save considerable time for the busy homemaker. It is a matter of forming the habit of folding clothes the simplest way and with the creases in the best places. See the illustration below for the perfect technique.

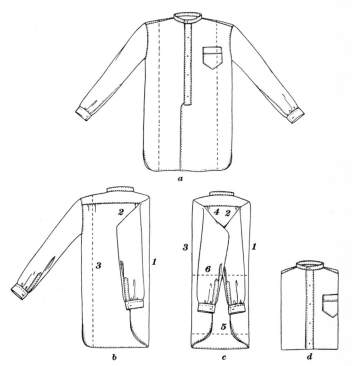

The process of folding a shirt. The first fold is lengthwise, as at 1, view *(b)*, the second turn places one of the sleeves, as at 2; the third is another lengthwise one, as at 3; and the fourth places the other sleeve as at 4, view *(c)*. Two more folds, as at 5 and 6, result in the folded shirt shown in view *(d)*.

HOME SEWING

Garments made at home usually cost less and wear better than store-bought styles. Disregarding the time spent in construction, you can usually buy material for less money than it takes to purchase a ready-to-wear garment of the same quality. Moreover, you can cut and make garments to fit you exactly.

USING PATTERNS. Many good magazines and stores offer patterns for sale. Some patterns are better than others. The simplest are usually the best, where the figure and its proportions have been kept in mind. Patterns are bought by measure; for example, a shirt may be ordered for a 34-inch bust measure.

A pattern is just like a puzzle—all the pieces fit together. It is wise to study all the pieces first; the parts are often numbered, and the description that goes with the pattern will tell the name of each piece. Observe the views shown on the outside of the envelope to see how you want to make your garment. Study the instruction sheet enclosed in the pattern envelope. It contains directions and diagrams for laying the pattern, cutting, and constructing the garment. Study and know the use of each marking before you use the pattern. Take your time; haste makes waste.

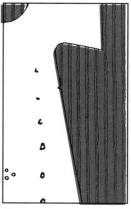

Using a pattern. Always study the pattern carefully before you begin. Lay each piece according to the instructions.

 In placing a pattern, as a rule the widest part of the pattern should be placed at the end of the cloth. This will be found most economical.

BEFORE YOU CUT. Fabric is expensive. Before carefully cutting cloth, decide which view on the pattern envelope you like and look at the table to determine how much material is required. Then, be sure to take the following precautions.

A couple treatments your fabric might require:

✂ *Preshrinking.* All fabrics have a tendency to shrink. Although shrinking has a tendency to detract from the "newness," often it is advisable to shrink material before cutting to ensure a better fit.

✂ *Straightening the ends of material.* Place the cloth, folded lengthwise on the table. Smooth out the material so that the end and selvedge follow the corner of the table. If one corner does not fall evenly on top of the other, the end of the material must be stretched into shape by pulling and stretching the shorter corner diagonally until the end is straight.

Textile Terms

selvedge	the finished edge
warp	the lengthwise threads
weft	the crosswise threads
bias	cutting the fabric on a diagonal
right side	the finished (top) side
wrong side	the unfinished (under) side
hand	the feel of a fabric

KNOWING YOUR SEWING MACHINE. One of the first things every homemaker should do is to learn about the sewing machine. Consult the instruction book. Open the machine, locate each part, and study its use. Learn how to wind a bobbin, to thread a bobbin case, to thread the machine. Know thoroughly how to use the machine; treat it as you would any delicate piece of machinery and it will give you good service.

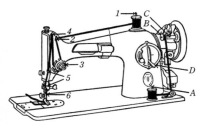

Parts of the sewing machine. 1. *Spool pin* — holds the thread. 2. *Thread guide* — holds the thread in place. 3. *Tension* — controls the tightness or looseness of the upper thread. 4. *Thread take-up* — moves up and down as a stitch is made carrying the thread to or from the tension. 5. *Thread guides* — hold the thread in place. 6. *Needle* — carries the upper thread. *Parts used in winding the bobbin:* A. *Spool pin* — holds the thread used in winding the bobbin; in some machines the two spool pins are side by side, B. *Bobbin* — part around which the lower thread is wound. C. *Bobbin winder* — part used in winding the thread from the spool onto the bobbin. D. *Stitch regulator.*

PROPER POSTURE COUNTS. Do you know that your stitching will be straighter and that you will tire less easily if you sit correctly at the sewing machine? Try the following position and see if it does not help:
✓ Place your chair straight in front of the machine.
✓ Sit squarely and erectly on your chair.
✓ Take a position so that your eyes are directly in line with the presser foot.

SEWING MACHINE CARE. A sewing machine, like all other machinery, will not give satisfaction unless kept clean and oiled. If used moderately, that is, only a few hours a day, cleaning and oiling once or twice a week is sufficient.

A few things to be careful about:
- Be sure that your machine is clean and well oiled; if it becomes sticky or if the machine is to stand unused for a few months, oil it. This will cleanse. Work it so that the oil will travel, and wipe off carefully. Consult the machine's manual for specific instructions.
- The thread, needle, and length of stitch must all be in keeping with the material. Consult the book or table of machine for size of needle to be used and suitable thread.
- If the machine does not work well and is in repair, it is generally because it is not threaded properly above or below the table, or perhaps the needle is blunt or has been incorrectly set. Examine these parts. If you cannot determine the problem, a trip to the repair shop may be in order.
- The table at the left hand is the place for the bulk of the work. It should not be crowded to the right of the presser foot, for it will then be impossible to guide the work easily or stitch well.

The qualities of good stitching are:
- Stitches of proper size and even in length. (For most materials, the stitches should be small; larger stitches may be better on very heavy material.)
- Thread matching the material in color, of the correct number, and a suitable kind (cotton or silk).
- Line of sewing straight.
- Stitches alike on both upper and under side.

THE ART OF SEWING BY HAND

Even if you sew your project on a machine, hand sewing is essential. A sewing basket in which to place the implements used for sewing is needed by every seamstress if she is to do her sewing easily.

The implements needed in the box are scissors or shears, measuring tape, needles, pin cushion, pins, thread, and thimble. In order to do good work, the implements must be of the right kind and in good condition. Following are explanations of the tools of the trade.

THE THIMBLE. Since the thimble is such an important tool, it should be selected carefully. A plastic thimble is thick and hence clumsy. A brass thimble discolors the finger. One of aluminum bends easily. Select a neatly made thimble of nickeled steel or silver that fits the second finger of the right hand.

How to use a thimble. Hold the point of the needle between thumb and first finger of the right hand, with the thimbled second finger against the eye. Take one stitch, and with the thimbled finger, push the needle entirely through. Practice.

PINS. For dressmaking, a pin should be slender, have a sharp point, and be made of a material that does not leave a stain on cloth. A supply of pins should be kept in a small box.

PIN CUSHION. The best pin cushion is stuffed with wool rather than cotton because needles and pins run through the wool much more easily than through the cotton.

SCISSORS AND SHEARS. Dull scissors or shears are an aggravation. For a good cutting edge that will retain its sharpness for some time, steel of good quality is necessary. It pays to buy scissors or shears of a high-grade metal, guaranteed by the manufacturer. Pinking shears are desirable for cutting materials that do not ravel readily, since seam edges may be both cut and finished in one operation. Scissors are six inches or less in length, while shears are over six inches in length. It is always best to buy shears when both cannot be purchased, because shears are always needed for cutting out garments.

MEASURING DEVICES. The very essential tape measure should be of cloth and measure 60 inches long and numbered on both sides, the numbers beginning at opposite ends of the two sides. The ends should be finished with metal pieces. A ruler 15 inches long with a reinforced metal edge is often a convenience. A yard-stick is very useful in placing a pattern on cloth and in determining a skirt length.

NEEDLES. Needles for hand sewing are made not only in different sizes, but in different lengths. Needles known as *sharps* are of medium length and are suitable for average sewing. For sewing on very fine materials, some prefer shorter. Needles  are of twelve sizes, the sizes being numbered from 1 to 12, the No. 12 being the finest. A package of needles may contain needles of different sizes or may contain needles all of one size. Sizes 8, 9, and 10 will be used the most.

SEWING THREAD. Basic sewing thread is made from cotton, linen, and silk. Cotton and linen thread are made in different sizes and are sold by number; the higher the number, the finer the thread.

 Reserve your best shears for fabric only. Paper will dull the blades rapidly.

SEAMS AND BASTING

The different pieces forming the garment are usually put together by means of a seam. *A seam is a line of sewing* (either hand or machine sewing) *joining two pieces.* In making a seam, it is well to pin the pieces of cloth together before basting. Most seams are sewed permanently by machine. Occasionally, seams are sewed by hand. Then either the running stitch or backstitch is used (see the illustrations on the facing page).

SEAM FINISHES. There are several methods of finishing a seam, most depending on the type of materials used in construction. (The illustrations below show each type.) For materials that do not ravel readily, the *pinking shears* make seam finishing easy. If the pinking shears are used in cutting a garment and the seams require no trimming, no additional seam finish is needed. For materials that ravel, *overcasting* is a satisfactory finish. For light-weight materials, seams may be finished by *edge-turning* and machine stitching. *Bound* stitching is often used for unlined coats, jackets, and slacks.

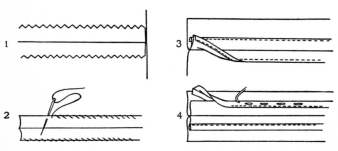

Plain Seam Finishes. 1. Pinked. 2. Overcast. 3. Edge turned and stitched. 4. Bound.

SELECTING THE PROPER SEAM FOR YOUR GARMENT. In making any garment, it is important to know what kind of seam should be used.

The most commonly used seams are:

* *Plain seam* — inconspicuous, flat (unless the finish makes it bulky).
* *Lapped seam* — conspicuous, less flat than a plain seam. Generally used in attaching a yoke to a garment and in joining a blouse and skirt. Sometimes used for skirt seams.
* *French seam* — inconspicuous, bulky if used on heavy materials.
* *Flat-fell seam* — conspicuous if machine finished; thick if used on heavy materials.

BASTING. Before you stitch a seam, it is important to pin and baste. Basting is *temporary* sewing, but it is *important* sewing. Although basting stitches are removed when a sewing process is completed, they are needed so that the permanent stitches may be well made. Sewing involves not only taking stitches, but holding the cloth in place so that the stitches may be made properly. Because basting stitches are larger than permanent sewing, cloth can be adjusted and held in place more easily when one is basting than when one is taking smaller stitches. Those who sew cleverly, baste skillfully.

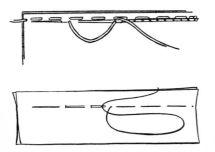

Backstitiching. Start with a running stitch. Then going back half a stitch, take another stitch. Continue with the latter stitch.

Running or basting stitch. Make sure the stitch is close and regular. For basting, the stitch length can be quite long.

HEMMING

Hemming is an extremely useful stitch. It can be used on many articles but especially for napery and the baby layette. To make a hem, the edge of the material is turned under ¼ inch or less. Then the material is folded a second time and basted. It is important that a gauge be used in folding a hem, so that the hem may be made even in width. Every thrifty homemaker should know how to hem. Table 10 shows the most common hand-sewn hemming stitches.

Steps in making a hem:
1. Mark the line of the hem. Stand on a table or fitting platform. The fitter measures up from the floor or table the number of inches the garment is to be from the floor when finished, using a yardstick or a tailor's square. She marks the hemline by a row of pins placed about three inches apart, parallel to the floor.
2. Fold the hem on line of pins to the wrong side and press.
3. Pin the fold with the heads of the pins up.
4. Baste the fold ¼ inch from the edge.
5. Test the hem's width with a marker or gauge; if uneven, mark an even line with tailor's chalk or pins and then trim on this line.
6. Turn in the raw edge ½ inch and crease.
7. Pin the edge of the hem to the garment, pinning the seams together first, then beginning at the center front and center back and pinning toward the seams.
8. Baste the hem to the garment with even bastings.
9. Finish the hem by hand or by machine stitching.
10. Remove all bastings.
11. Press carefully.

Table 10. Hemming Stitches

1. *Slant hemming.* Small slanting stitches, used for narrow hems.

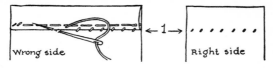

2. *Vertical hemming.* Small straight stitches, less conspicuous than slant hemming stitches.

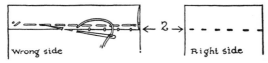

3. *Slip stitching.* Stitches barely visible on both sides, used for shirt hems and facings.

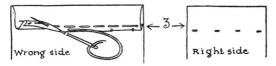

4. *Catch stitching.* Work from left to right, used for hems of lined coats and curtains.

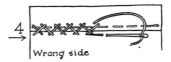

5. *Machine edge stitching and hand hemming or slip stitching.* Used for skirt hems and facings.

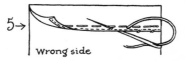

REUSING BITS OF FABRIC

A handmade laundry bag is a fun, easy project for even the most novice sewer. Figure A (right) shows how the bag can be cut from one yard of 48-inch fabric. Smaller bags can be cut from any leftover material you have on hand. The size of the bag can be planned to suit your needs. It can even be used to hold a special gift. Waste not, want not!

Laundry bag with drawstring:

1. Make a four-inch hem across the top of the bag (Fig. *B*). (See pages 108–109 for making hems.) Press. Then make a line of stitching 1½ inches from the top to form a casing for the drawstring. Retrace the ends.
2. Fold the bag in half (Fig. *C*), right sides together, and make a ½-inch seam across the bottom and up one side. Press.
3. Reinforce the top of the seam at the hemline by stitching across the open seam just below the hemline (Fig. *D*).
4. Make a drawstring of material and put through the casing.
5. Finish the bag neatly. Remove all bastings, pins, and hanging threads. Give a final pressing.

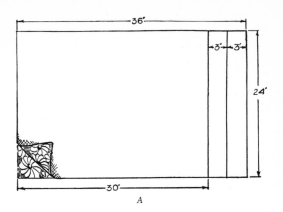

A

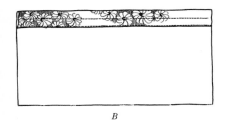

B

C

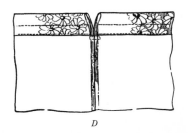

D

MENDING

"A stitch in time saves nine," and the life of an article of clothing may be prolonged by good care. This means that if you take one stitch to mend a small hole, it will save nine stitches in mending a large hole. This in turn means more money to spend on other things when one's income is limited.

Mend all worn places in clothing as soon as you discover them. This makes mending easier, saves time, makes the garment last longer, and makes the mended place show less. A garment always looks better and lasts longer if holes are mended when they are small. To keep your clothing in good repair means that you keep trimmings and fasteners sewed on, stitch ripped seams, darn worn places, patch holes in any article of clothing, and press them carefully. Repairing, skillfully done, does not detract from the appearance of clothing.

DARNING AND PATCHING. The kind of tear or worn spot determines whether the hole should be mended by darning or patching. If the edges of the hole are not raveled and no cloth has been torn out of the garment, darn it. A tear can be darned the least conspicuously by using ravelings of the cloth and mending on the wrong side. If it is impossible to get ravelings, use thread as near the color of the cloth as possible.

To strengthen a torn spot, it is often advisable to baste a small piece of cloth underneath the tear and darn through the two thicknesses of cloth. The running stitch should be used. The stitches should run in the same direction as the lengthwise or crosswise threads of the garment.

 Lost buttons or holes in stockings or other garments do not look neat. No one wishes to be unattractive in appearance. Mend today!

Darning. In darning, the hole is replaced by interlacing threads, as in weaving. It is a simple way to repair worn garments and to prevent tears. Only the smaller holes should be darned; larger ones are patched.

Darning is generally done by hand. Select crewel needles in keeping with the thread. The thread should match the threads of the material. For an inconspicuous darn, ravel some threads of the material being darned. If a raveling thread cannot be obtained, use a mercerized thread of the same color and weight.

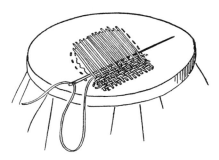

An embroidery hoop helps keep the fabric taut for darning.

To darn a worn or thin place:
1. Put the worn place in an embroidery hoop or, if the garment being darned is a stocking, put it over a darner.
2. Put in lengthwise rows of running stitches beginning back from the sides of the worn place, so that it is reinforced, making the rows of running stitches about a thread apart and of uneven length.
3. Turn the mended place and make the crosswise running stitches about a thread apart and of uneven length.

Patching. Patching is filling a hole with new material. A good patch always has the warp and woof (weft) threads of the patch match these same threads in the garment. The figures of the garment and patch must also match. If given careful attention and small stitches are taken, it is possible to patch a garment so that it is scarcely noticeable.

Materials needed:
✓ Patch of same material as the garment.
✓ Thread of suitable color and size to make inconspicuous stitches. Fine thread is least noticeable.
✓ No. 8 or 9 needle; thimble.

Steps in making a patch:
1. Trim the edges of the hole so that it is square or rectangular.
2. Place a piece of material underneath the hole so that the threads of the patch and garment run in the same direction and the figures match (if there are any). Pin the patch in place.
3. Trim the edges of the patch so that it extends 1 inch beyond the outline of the hole. Baste.
4. Hand hem or machine stitch the patch.

TO SEW ON A SNAP. If you examine the two parts of a snap, you will see that there is a ball in the center of one, and a socket in the center of the other. One part of a snap is sewed to the wrong side of the lapped-over edge, and the other part is sewed to the right side of the lapped-under edge. It is important that the ball part be sewed on the lapped-over edge. If the socket part is sewed to this edge, the underside of the socket often wears a hole in the garment, especially if the garment is laundered often. The method of attaching each part is shown in the illustration on the facing page.

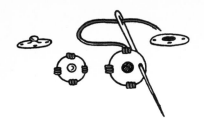

To attach a snap. Use thicker thread or finer thread doubled. Through each hole, take at least three stitches. Fasten securely.

TO SEW ON A BUTTON. Follow these easy steps for attaching any type of button.

1. Using a double thread, take a fastening stitch on the right side.
2. Bring the needle through a hole in the button and down through the opposite hole.
3. Placing a pin under the thread on top of the button, take several stitches over the pin to securely fasten the button. Buttons with two holes should have the stitches running parallel to the button-hole, while buttons with four holes may have the stitches form a cross or parallel stitches on the right side.
4. Remove the pin and twist the thread several times around the stitches between the button and the cloth. This forms a shank that protects the stitches and makes enough room for the button in the buttonhole.

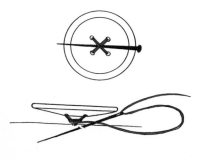

To attach a button. After placing a pin under thread, and making several stitches, remove the pin, and wind the thread around the threads holding the button in place.

"Whatever your income may be, see to it
that the home is yours, that it sends a breath
of your personality, that its hangings and
touches are natural, and not a replica
of your neighbor across the way."

Management and Furnishings of the Home

Have you noticed how some homes look and feel *homey*, like they are a comfortable and clean place to live? Any home can be made sunny and attractive, however simple or splendid it may be, if one knows how. It can be done even though one has little money if one has right ideals and if one understands how to get pleasing effects.

In a real home, every member of a family enjoys every room. Good home atmosphere is provided by making every room attractive and convenient. Every part of a house should be usable, affording comfort and pleasure according to its purpose. Such a place may be called a home. It is not the result of a hurried purchase of a load of furniture, but comes only with years of planning and thoughtful experience. The homemaking studies teach how to make the house attractive, how to manage it in such a way that the money or income is wisely spent. It means learning to do the household work systematically and well—in short, it means creating a cheerful, bright, homey place.

THE JOY OF HOMEOWNERSHIP

The important thing for the homemaker to know is how to select a house that will be sanitary and comfortable to live in. One enjoys a home mainly because of two reasons: first, that rest, food, and entertainment are always there for oneself; and second, that the same is provided for one's guests. And one cannot rest in or enjoy conditions that are not salutary.

When inspecting a home for living, consider good air circulation and sunshine; don't be distracted by unimportant details. Sometimes people forget to look ahead and think only of whether the house has a beautiful entrance or an elevator. If one must choose between such things and good air, light, and sunshine, choose the latter. Also, it is always wise and pays in the long run to have a plumber test the pipes, in case there may be leaks or foul gases that will injure health; this is especially true in an old house. You might also have the locale thoroughly fumigated, for one does not always know who the previous occupants of the house may have been and whether it has been kept clean and in good order.

MONETARY CONSIDERATIONS. Owning a home brings responsibilities. Although more homes than not are bought with a mortgage, there is usually an outlay of cash, for an initial payment must invariably be made. Then, too, repairs must be taken care of by the owner of a house. These must be factored in from the outset.

On the other hand, there are many advantages in owning a home. Living in one's own home gives one a feeling of security and permanence. There is so much more incentive to improve the house, to beautify the lawn, to have a garden. A home is a means of expressing personality. Some families find that such pleasure more than compensates for the responsibilities of home owning.

When buying a home, keep these points in mind:

- ♠ There should always be a down payment. The balance of the amount is paid in monthly installments over a period of years.
- ♠ When purchasing a ready-built house, buy one built by a reputable builder or have the construction examined by a reliable person who understands building.
- ♠ Having a reliable contractor responsible for building the entire house gives the owner more assurance as to the final cost of the house.
- ♠ A family planning to build a house should have definite information about the cost of wallpaper, window shades, curtain rods, and any such furnishing which must be purchased for a new house.

A WORD OF WARNING. The amount of money that one has to spend on a home usually determines the kind and location of a home. It is wise to invest in a piece of property, whether in the city or country, only after one has taken time to become thoroughly acquainted with it.

A prospective homeowner should be cautious. There are many families who have had heart-breaking experiences in attempting to own homes, such as:

Cost of the house being too great — The payments were so large that they became an excessive burden.

Too small a down payment being made — Interest charges were therefore large and payments on the principal exceedingly small.

Poor construction — House repairs were frequent and costly.

A home should be on high ground, if possible. High ground makes for good scenery and dry cellars.

QUALITIES OF A GOOD HOME. This idea must be kept in mind as one begins to plan: What kind of home do I wish to create? The right kind of atmosphere makes one happy and is conducive to better living. Plenty of fresh air and sunshine make for healthy surroundings. Very often even high-priced homes are so very close together that no sunshine and very little light can possibly get in. Such a condition is not desirable.

Everyone loves beautiful surroundings, so it is only fair to select for a home a site that is reached by attractive streets. Natural views always make a home more beautiful and greatly increase the value of a property. Ideally, a home should also be near schools and places of worship, a grocery and pharmacy, and public transportation. Convenience of a site is measured by the distance to work, schools, and shopping centers, not so much in miles but in the time that it takes to reach there.

A well-painted house of pleasing lines and a neatly kept lawn are something to be proud of.

SALUBRITY AND SUNSHINE. Sunlight does little good for a home unless there are plenty of windows where it can enter. With the possible exception of a bathroom, there should be at least two windows in each room. If the windows are on adjacent or opposite sides of a room, ventilation will be better. A damp room is not a fit place to live in at any time. To ensure adequate air and sunshine, make a floor plan of the home or apartment showing the layout of rooms and placement of windows. Good air circulation is vital to health, and health is the most important thing in life for which one can plan.

Sunshine in a room destroys disease and does away with mental depression sooner than any drugs. Good ventilation helps dislodge the little beast, the microbe.

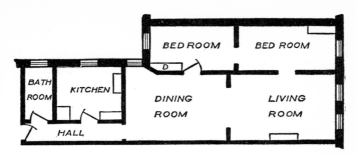

Making a floor plan of your house or apartment will help you furnish and decorate.

ROOMS IN THE HOUSE. The size and number of rooms are important considerations in choosing a house. Each room in the house should be a unit, with every line, shape, tone, and color taking its place in an orderly scheme. The living room should present an appearance of warmth and inviting quiet. Bedrooms should be airy and cool, with the simplest of furnishing. The kitchen should be light and convenient, with as good an equipment as a workman would demand in a modern shop. Inexpensive homes, where much floor space is impossible, may be better with one large room as a combination living and dining room rather than with two small rooms.

The living room: If the living room is to give the feeling of rest and comfort, it will never be overdecorated and will be furnished as a livable room in which one may use everything in it every day. It should never be formal because it is the room where we live. Comfortable chairs, with books and magazines conveniently placed, invite one to rest and read. Perhaps the room may need a bit of bright color in a floor pillow or a table runner, which you can easily make.

Since our living rooms are for use and not for show, we want them to be comfortable. We want them simply furnished so that they will be easy to keep fresh and clean. We want the colors on walls and floors to be restful and pleasing. We want no unnecessary ornaments or furniture.

The table in the living room should be large enough to be useful. It need not be expensive, but it should be spotless, of a convenient size, and well placed. If a desk is in the living room, it must be placed so that light will fall over the writer's left shoulder from window by day and from lamp by night. The comfort of every member of the family who uses the living room should be looked after.

The dining room. The dining room should always express a cheerful and hospitable atmosphere. Generally the dining table is placed in the center of the room so the family and friends may be grouped about it. Remember that natural flowers, when attractively arranged, add beauty in any room, especially to the dining table.

A dining room containing a normal-sized dining table should be at least 11 feet wide. This width gives enough space for the person waiting on the table to pass between chairs and wall. The dining room should adjoin or be very close to the kitchen. The walls should be finished in light colors rather than dark, which tend to make the room appear gloomy. The window curtains should be of a kind easily laundered, since draperies in a dining room are apt to hold dirt and odors and need frequent cleaning. The floor is best made of hardwood, for a rug may then be used instead of a carpet. A dining-room floor would be more sanitary if no covering were used, but the noise made by using a bare floor is annoying to many persons.

Bedrooms and clothes closets: In a family where there are both boys and girls, there should be at least three bedrooms—one for the mother and father, one for the boys, and one for the girls. In homes with plenty of rooms, there is often a bedroom for each one of the children. Having a special guest room makes it pleasant to entertain friends overnight without disturbing the family. It is advisable to consider not only the size of a bedroom and the number of windows but also its clothes closet. Closet space is always important in choosing a place to live, for one should be able to put one's belongings out of sight and to keep them free from dust.

Bathrooms: A bathroom should be easily accessible to the bedrooms. It should not be necessary to pass through another room to reach a bathroom. Since a bathroom requires very frequent cleaning, its walls and floors should be of easily washable material, such as tile. Cupboards or drawers for towels and washcloths are a convenience.

Kitchen: Since the kitchen is used mainly for the preparation and cooking of food and for the washing and storing of dishes and utensils, its equipment should be grouped to form these three centers:

1. *A food-preparation center.* This comprises a work table with cupboards suitable for storing staple food supplies and utensils, a refrigerator, and a sink close by.
2. *A cooking center.* A stove with a nearby cupboard for storing utensils needed when cooking from this unit.
3. *A dishwasher,* or dishwashing center.

 The large articles of furniture, such as piano, bookcase, buffet, bed, and dresser, are the most difficult articles to place. Before going house-hunting, it is wise to measure and make a note of the dimensions of the large pieces.

INTERIOR DESIGN

The day has passed when harmonious lines and pleasing colors are found only in homes of the extremely wealthy. The present-day homemaker, loving her home, longs to make it cheery and beautiful—a place where those dear to her enjoy lingering, and her friends delight in coming.

The services of the professional decorator may, of course, be secured, but the home best loved is the home where the taste and ideas of the homemaker strike the personal note. Whatever your income may be, see to it that the home is yours, that it sends a breath of your personality, that its hangings and touches are natural, and not a replica of your neighbor across the way or two streets over.

Home should be a place where we can be comfortable and happy. The house and all that furnishes it should be planned with this idea in mind. Unless a thing contributes to our comfort, happiness, or both, it is worthless, and we cannot afford to give it space, even in the attic or cellar.

COLOR. The first thing to do when entering any new space is to study the rooms as a whole and consider the color of walls in relation to the floors, woodwork, and ceiling. As a rule one should expect to find the darkest tones underfoot and a gradation of color up to the ceiling. In small houses or apartments it is a good rule to have the same treatment of walls, floors, and woodwork in rooms that open into one another. Notice what an appearance of spaciousness this treatment gives.

UNITY AND SIMPLICITY. The first guiding principle in the selection of decorations and furnishings for a home is unity. Some definite scheme should be adopted in planning the whole apartment or house. This idea should be kept always in mind when the decorations and furnishings are selected.

Simplicity of line, harmony, and decoration must be your watch-words. Guard carefully that nothing grotesque creeps into your picture. Simplicity in house decoration and furnishing is evidence of good taste. One picture of a good print and simple framing will be preferable to several bright ones or large family portraits in gilt moldings; one simple vase with a beautiful spray of apple blossoms or daisies has more beauty than an exhibition of bric-a-brac, such as many homes exhibit.

Strive for a simple, unified design rather than ostentatious display, and always choose fine quality over poor reproductions.

APPROPRIATENESS. Avoid the selection of unusual or pretentious furnishings or decoration. The furnishings should represent the ideals and the standards of living of the family and should be within the family's income. Ideals as well as ideas influence selection. Simple wicker furniture and muslin curtains, if one can afford them, are better than cheap imitations of fancy brocaded satin draperies and upholstered chairs. The principle of appropriateness must be borne in mind in the furnishing of each room.

If a room is gloomy and poorly lighted because it has few windows, a light wall color of yellow or cream will produce a very bright effect; this effect is due to reflection of light as well as decoration.

THE SPECIAL LITTLE TOUCHES

Accessories, the smaller articles of home furnishings, such as lamps, pictures, and pillows, add much to the livable atmosphere of a home. Without some ornaments, a home seems barren, yet too many make a room feel cluttered. Be certain that the pieces chosen are useful, beautiful in themselves, and in harmony with the rest of the room.

MIRRORS. The property of reflecting objects of pleasing shape and color makes a mirror an interesting wall decoration. A mirror placed over a mantel or opposite a doorway makes a room appear larger.

TEXTILES FOR WALLS AND FLOORS. There are many cotton, linen, rayon, and silk textiles of interesting color and design, and some of these make charming wall decorations. If floor coverings must be used, know that carpets are never sanitary because they cannot easily be removed or cleansed. It is always more sanitary to have bare floors and to use rugs, or even to have bare floors without rugs.

LIGHTING. A lighted lamp is very conspicuous. For this reason alone, it should be attractive and suitably decorative. The light or lamp should produce eye comfort. Extreme contrasts in light are bad; very dark areas and very bright ones adjacent are not pleasing. The light fixture should be as much a part of the room as the textiles, the carpet, or the furniture. Shades and reflectors are used to improve lamps by decreasing the brilliancy of the illuminant; controlling the distribution of light; softening shadows, lessening contrasts; and giving

Distributing   Concentrating

some decorative effect. A shade is a device for changing the intensity of a light; a reflector for changing the distribution of the light. The two most common are *(a)* the distributing (for general lighting) and *(b)* the concentrating types and (for task lighting).

DISHES. Select a style with simple decoration or without decoration. Large conspicuous designs and bright colors become tiresome when the dishes are used often. A good-quality undecorated china is a wise choice, for any type of decorated dish looks well with it.

PILLOWS AND BLANKETS. Select pillows that are attractive but always practical. A fancy pillow that cannot be used has no place in a home. The ideal blanket is one that is light in weight, but warm. Wool, especially virgin wool, is a good textile for blankets. Because of its elasticity, air is enclosed between the fibers during the weaving process. The enclosed air helps to make the blanket warm.

FABRICS AND TABLE LINENS. Buy fabrics of good quality, as they will wear better, and keep the design simple. Remember that simplicity in design and beauty in fabric are two essentials of artistic linens. White linen tablecloths and napkins are better to buy than cotton, because linen wears longer and launders much better than cotton.

TOWELS. The loops on the surface of a bath towel make it absorb water more readily. Long loops close together absorb more water than shorter loops farther apart.

 It is dangerous to add layer upon layer of paper to walls; vermin often collect, as well as germs of disease. If used, it must be carefully cleansed by being rubbed down occasionally with a clean cloth. Paint is the most sanitary wall covering, for it can be scrubbed with soap and water.

SELECTION OF FURNISHINGS

The type of household furnishings should correspond with the home in which they are to be used. It is one of the signs of good taste to have the furnishings in keeping with the other surroundings. Three important requirements for home furnishings are that they be simple, useful, and artistic. Suitable furnishings help to make a house a home.

TAKE YOUR TIME. Furnishing a home takes time. Have a definite plan and a harmonious scheme in view, and know how much you can afford to spend. As you select or aid in the selection of useful and attractive furnishings for your scheme, it will be of value to consider these questions:

- Do the furnishings present a unified appearance with the background of a room?
- Are the furnishings suited to the type of home?
- Are the furnishings of the same general type?
- Is there a pleasing general color scheme?
- Is each room furnished so that it seems a part of the house?
- Is each room furnished to serve its purpose?
- Are the furnishings of every room comfortable and convenient?
- Are only the necessary furnishings used, thus avoiding too much bric-a-brac?
- Are they of the best quality possible for the money spent?

DESIGN, COLOR, AND USE. The same basic principles of design and of color for clothes may be applied to furniture. A piece of furniture should be appropriate in size for the room or the space in which it is to be placed. Its design should harmonize with (not necessarily match) other articles of furniture. Furniture should not only be pleasing to look at, but it should be practical, serving a real purpose.

LARGE VERSUS SMALL FURNITURE. The charm of many small homes is destroyed by furniture that is too large for the rooms in which it is placed. In buying new or used furniture, or in assembling furniture from different parts of the home, the size of the furniture should be considered. Articles of furniture should also be of suitable size for the wall spaces against which they are to be placed.

ARRANGING FURNITURE. Often a room may be improved not by buying new furnishings but by rearranging those we have. In arranging furniture, the larger pieces should be placed parallel to the wall, not diagonally across a corner. In some cases it is pleasing to place a rectangular living-room table with the shorter, rather than the longer, sides parallel to the wall. The large pieces of furniture should be distributed around the room so that no side of a room appears more heavily weighted than another.

Consider balance and proportion when arranging furniture and accessories.

Since the bed is the largest piece of furniture in a bedroom, it is well to determine its position first. If possible, place the bed so that the light from a window will not shine in the eyes. Also, place the bed so that there is some unoccupied wall space on each side of it. Do not, if avoidable, push the side of a bed against a wall.

WOOD FURNITURE. Wood furniture is made either of solid wood or of a foundation wood over which one or more thin layers of wood are glued. Such wood is called *veneer*. Veneer is usually wood of beautiful grain.

Furniture is often advertised as having a maple, walnut, or mahogany finish on hard wood. Of course, such furniture is not maple, walnut, or mahogany. It is made of less-prized wood stained to imitate these more expensive woods. Imitations of choice woods may serve one's needs, but it is not thrifty to pay choice-wood prices for imitations. In buying furniture, it is wise to be able to recognize woods by their grains. If you are not sure of your ability to do this, ask the salesperson.

A room containing furniture of more than one kind of wood may be more pleasing than one with furniture of the same kind of wood. The woods, however, should be somewhat similar in grain. Because mahogany and walnut are both fine grained, they look well together. Oak and mahogany are usually not a pleasing combination.

Legs: Chair, cabinet, and table legs, as well as bedposts, should be examined for sturdiness. Straight legs or posts that are sawed from a single board are usually satisfactory. But a curved leg or post made from a single board may not be sufficiently strong. The latter may split if there is a short length of grain at any point. Heavy furniture legs and posts are sometimes made of several length-wise strips of wood glued together. If the gluing is well done, such legs are strong.

Joints: The framework of furniture should be investigated. Sturdy joints are shown in the illustrations below. A joint held together by nails and glue is not strong enough to stand much strain.

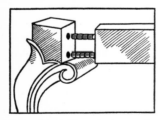

A dowel joint. The spiral grooved wooden pin or dowel is covered with glue and driven into the hole in the block.

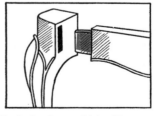

Mortised and tenoned joint. The mortise is the rectangular hole, the tenon is the rectangular projection. The latter is covered with glue and driven into the hole.

Drawers: A drawer that is not sturdy and does not slide easily is an aggravation. Well-made drawers have: (1) Side joints dovetailed, not merely grooved and glued or nailed. (2) The bottom joined to the sides by grooving. (3) One or more blocks glued underneath to each side to hold the bottom and sides securely. (4) A center or side drawer-glide (a center glide is preferable). (5) A dust-proof partition between the drawers.

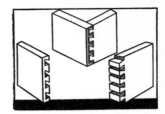

An example of dovetailed joints.

Springs: The most satisfactory springs are made of tempered steel. The greater the number of springs on a chair seat, the more durable the seat. Over the springs there should be a covering of burlap or heavy cotton material. Next is the stuffing. Over the stuffing is a layer of cotton. The qualities of the outer covering of furniture should be considered carefully. Only durable textiles, such as wool or high-grade cotton, should be used.

OLD FURNITURE MADE OVER. The art of making over, or combining several pieces of furniture, and changing same, is within reach of all. An old table, canapé, etc., with varnish scraped off, can be ornamented with flowers, scrolls, or figures painted on in strongly contrasting colors. A mirror taken from an old dresser and hung by colored cord over the top of same, the whole done over to suit the coloring of a room, beautifies many a space at very little expense.

THE SCIENCE OF COLOR

We all love color, but too riotous a display of inharmonious color hurts. Decorative ideas are brought on by color harmony. As we all know, primary colors are red, blue, and yellow. Mix all three, and a brownish grey results. Mix any two and the resulting color is the complementary. The experience of color-educated persons must be taken as the basis of judgment of harmony, and the table shown on the facing page attempts to express concretely such judgments.

Complementary colors are important from an artistic point of view since they offer the greatest possible contrast to each other. In the chromatic circle below, the colors opposite each other are complementary.

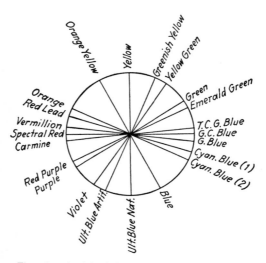

The color wheel can help you in all aspects of your life,
including decorating your home.

Table 11. Color Harmonies

Crimson and orange	Bad
Crimson and yellow	Inferior
Crimson and green	Strong but harsh
Crimson and blue	Good
Crimson and violet	Bad
Crimson and gold-yellow	Good
Scarlet and yellow	Bad
Scarlet and green	Inferior
Scarlet and greenish-blue	Good
Scarlet and blue	Good
Scarlet and violet	Bad
Orange and yellow	Poor
Orange and yellow-green	Fair
Orange and green	Strong—poor
Orange and green-blue	Fair
Orange and blue	Good
Orange and violet	Strong—good
Orange-yellow and crimson	Poor
Orange-yellow and scarlet	Poor
Orange-yellow and green	Bad
Orange-yellow and blue-green	Bad
Orange-yellow and green-blue	Fairly good
Orange-yellow and blue	Excellent
Orange-yellow and violet	Good
Yellow and crimson	Poor
Yellow and green	Bad
Yellow and blue-green	Very bad
Yellow and blue	Fair
Yellow and violet	Very good
Green and blue	Very poor
Green and violet	Moderate
Green and red	Good

DECORATING THE SMALL APARTMENT

There are as many ways of decorating our rooms as there are of dressing ourselves that detract from poor points and emphasize good ones. Such considerations are especially important when dealing with a small space. The homemaker who lives in an apartment should follow a few simple rules for decoration that make living in an apartment a real delight from every point of view.

1. The walls should be plain and restfully neutral, preferably done in pale cream and gray tints, the warmer tones being used in darker rooms, the gray tones in sunny ones. All these tones should melt into the general scheme, showing no startling difference. When the apartment is inclined to be dark, pale yellowy creams should be used entirely, with the warm sunny colors in the draperies.

2. Mirrors supply an effect of spaciousness and light. Mirrored panels may be set into walls with narrow moldings, French fashion. Do not place them directly opposite each other, as such reflections prove confusing; they should be planned to reflect decorative bits of the opposite unmirrored wall.

3. Since apartment houses are intentionally impersonal, owing to the varied personalities they must shelter, it is very necessary that a homelike atmosphere greets the opening of the door. Comfortably informal furniture, happy draperies, soft-shaded lamps, gleaming candles, books, flowers, an open fire—these achieve the personality of home.

4. The floors should be dark and laid with large, unobtrusively colored rugs, showing little pattern. The hangings and occasional bit of upholstery may be of bold design, toned down by a restful background. Since rooms are so close, the color scheme of the entire apartment should be planned from a one-room standpoint.

5. The furniture, of course, should not be massive and should be convertible, serving more than one purpose. In the living room, a day bed may take the place of a sofa, and when its day cover and up-to-the-minute pillows are removed, snowy sheets and fleecy blankets are revealed for the delectation of the overnight guest. The table and desk may be satisfactorily combined in the Chippendale table desk with drawer space on each side. If the dining room is combined with the living room, a gateleg table takes the place of a living and dining table, and the secretaire desk may hold china behind its small-paned doors.

Convertible furniture that serves more than one function is perfect for the apartment or small space.

6. Build shelves for books. Nests of tables and drop-leaf tables save space; a lowboy pushed against a wall may be used to hold another lamp, with the advantage of additional drawer and shelf space below. Upholstered furniture should be daintily designed.

7. In the bedroom, space should be given to "real" pieces—chests, chiferobes, bureaus—if there is not room for the entire suite, and this especially when there is a man to be considered.

When ceilings are low, one should never use borders of paper but should carry the wall decoration to the ceiling. Striped paper helps to accentuate the height of a room.

A CLEAN HOUSE IS INVITING

A home may be very plain; its furnishings, the most inexpensive sort; its colors ill-chosen. However, if it is clean and orderly, there is something inviting about it. To be sure, cleanliness is by no means the only thing that makes a home inviting, but it is an important factor.

CLEAN, HEALTHY LIVING. Cleanliness is important, not only for appearance and comfort, but for health. Dust and dirt may contain particles of stone, brick, decayed matter, and also germs. Some of the germs cause disease, while others cause changes or decay in food, wood, cloth, etc. Some of these changes are helpful, while others are undesirable. As it is better to keep the house clean than to clean house, take the following precautions:

✓ Keep walks, steps, porches, etc., clean.
✓ Keep insects out by screening doors and windows. Keep food, garbage, etc., covered.
✓ Have no unnecessary dust-collecting surfaces; for example, window casings and door frames should not have horizontal grooves.
✓ Avoid accumulating unnecessary articles that require constant dusting. Be too clean to clutter.
✓ Clean regularly and systematically.

PLANNING HOUSEHOLD WORK. There is no one plan of running a house that will be satisfactory for all households. Schedules are dependent upon such factors as the size of the home, the number of members in the family and their ages, the amount of dust or soot in a community, and the family income. For example, in some localities it is necessary to wash windows once a week; in other places once every month is sufficient. Table 12 shows plans that suited one home. Although they may not prove satisfactory in your home, they offer suggestions.

Table 12. Plan of Household Work

TO DO EVERY DAY

- Straighten up and dust living room, dining room, and bedrooms
- Wash dishes, sink, stove
- Put away dishes
- Empty waste baskets

- Straighten up kitchen cupboards
- Make beds
- Sweep kitchen
- Empty garbage

TO DO TWICE A WEEK

- Clean kitchen and bathroom thoroughly
- Evaluate refrigerator and cupboards for shopping needs
- Sweep outdoor porches and walkways

TO DO ONCE A WEEK

- Launder, iron, and put away clothes
- Clean living room, dining room, bedrooms, and hall thoroughly
- Clean laundry and basement
- Change bed linens

TO DO ONCE A MONTH (OR MORE OFTEN)

- Clean kitchen and dining-room cupboards or buffet
- Wash windows (more often if the air is sooty)
- Wash mirrors

- Polish silver or plate
- Polish brass candlesticks or other articles
- Wash piano keys
- Clean dresser drawers

TO DO EVERY SIX MONTHS

- Wash or clean woodwork
- Brush or dry-clean draperies
- Wash painted walls

TO DO ONCE A YEAR

- Clean papered walls with wallpaper cleaner
- Beat carpets or large rugs

CLEANING EACH ROOM. If a home is to be kept orderly and clean, there is work that must be done daily. The living room, dining room, and other bedrooms should be aired, cleaned, arranged, and dusted. Following are other cleaning tips for each room in your house.

Bedrooms: The secret of keeping a bedroom in good order and using as little time as possible in its care is to have a definite place for everything. Besides putting away clothes and other belongings, you must remember that bedrooms need frequent dusting.

We spend nearly a third of our lives in our bedroom. It should be both attractive and sanitary. The bedroom has as few draperies as possible. The curtains are light in weight, easily washed, and easily pushed back from the windows. The floor is kept as clean as possible. The covering of the floor should be easily cleaned if the floor is not of bare wood. The furniture should be plain so it, too, can be easily and quickly cleaned.

People sometimes are so anxious to have the room look orderly that they do not allow for the proper airing of the bed linen. When it is thoroughly fresh, then is the time to put it back neatly upon the mattress. When the bed is neatly made, a room takes on a tidy appearance. To do a neat piece of work in bed-making one must be sure that the sheets and other coverings are: Clean. Straight. Smooth.

Right side up, spread the sheet over the bed, wider hem at top. Miter the corners by grasping the edge and lifting the hand so that a diagonal fold *AB* is made at the corner. Tuck *CD* under the mattress.

 A mattress pad should be laid over the mattress to give added softness and protection.

By changing pillow slips and sheets once a week, a bed can usually be kept reasonably clean. To get bed covers on straight, two points should be observed: the center lengthwise fold should be in the center and the overhang along the two sides should be equal. To arrange bed covers smoothly, corners of the sheets and other covers should be mitered.

Living room: First, it must always be neat. Of course this means clean. But it also means that if there are any plants or flowers in the room, they are always kept fresh. Magazines and books are placed in order on the table. The writing desk is always tidy. The room is aired every day so that if the air has been spoiled by tobacco smoke, it may be freshened again.

Bathrooms: The bathroom is the test of good housekeeping. Keep the bathroom clean and orderly. Regularly wipe the faucets, sink, and tub. Clean the mirror, wash the drinking glass, supply fresh soap and toilet paper, and put up clean wash cloths and towels. Each member of the family should have his or her own towel and washcloth. There should be some way of identifying each—a towel bar for each member, or a definite place on a rack assigned to each person.

Always leave the bathroom as clean and as orderly as you would like to find it. Where several members of the family use the same bathroom, each one must leave the tub or the basin spotlessly clean. Besides the necessary daily cleaning, on the weekly cleaning day, wipe down the walls; sweep and mop the floor; clean the medicine cabinet; thoroughly clean the sink, tub, and closet; polish.

The Kitchen: The kitchen should be the most orderly and sanitary room in the house because much of the work takes place in it and the food is prepared there. If you have time to clean only one room, make it this one.

If there are grease spots from the sputtering of something on the stove, this should be wiped off just after it has happened; the painted ceiling and wall must be washed off with a piece of cloth wrung out from warm water or softened with a small quantity of cleaner. The kitchen paint is washed in the same way.

Essential steps in clearing a table and washing the dishes:

1. Remove, scrape, rinse, sort, and pile the dishes.
2. Wash the dishes in hot, soapy water. Rinse, and wipe. *First*, wash the glasses. Polish them with a clean towel. Be sure lint is not left on them. Put them away without touching them with your fingers. Do you like to see finger marks on glassware? *Second*, wash the silver. It must be wiped dry. *Third*, wash the cups and saucers, plates, and other serving dishes. Rinse and wipe dry. *Fourth*, wash the pots and pans. Rinse well and dry carefully. If you don't have too many dishes, place the dishes in a rack to dry.
3. Wash the kitchen table, drain board, and sink.
4. See that the dish cloth and tea towels are left clean. It is well to rinse them very frequently in hot water and to wash them two or three times a week in hot, soapy water.

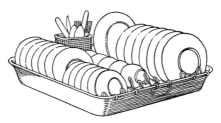

A dish rack helps the washed dishes dry faster as well as protect the dishes from breaking.

EFFICIENCY IN CLEANING

If all the work that needs to be done in a home is listed and scheduled for certain days or parts of days, and the time is noted and motions studied in doing each piece of work, the running of a household can be made much more efficient.

It is easy to waste time and energy in doing work because:

* Steps in doing a piece of work are not planned and consequently are not followed in the proper order.
* The right tool is not used. The tools and materials are not collected and conveniently placed before doing a piece of work.
* The worker is not in a comfortable position while doing the work.
* The kind of work or movement is changed too often. If possible, keep on with one kind of work or motion until it is finished.

Rules for Sweeping and Dusting

SWEEPING	DUSTING
1. Cover all food before sweeping.	1. Use a soft cloth for dusting and one that will not leave lint or threads.
2. Never sweep while food is being prepared or served.	2. Fold the dust into the cloth while working to avoid scattering dust, and use a clean part of the duster for each article.
3. Begin sweeping at one corner or side of the room and sweep toward the center.	3. A slightly dampened duster may be used on painted surfaces.
4. Use short strokes, keeping the broom close to the floor.	4. Dust high places first.
5. If possible, sweep in the direction in which the floorboards are laid.	5. Avoid shaking the duster.
6. The broom should be stroked away from the one sweeping, to avoid scattering dust on the worker.	6. Wash duster after using.
7. Gather the dirt in small piles.	7. Use a slightly oiled duster on polished surfaces.
8. Use alternate sides of the broom in order that broom may wear evenly.	8. A dry duster should be used for surfaces of leather, glass, etc.

OCCASIONAL CLEANING

Whether the cleaning is weekly, monthly, or seasonal, some suggestions for cleaning the walls, floors, and furnishings will help to make the work easier and save your time.

WINDOWS. A window defeats its purpose if it is not clean and clear. If a window is very dirty, wipe it first with a soft cloth. Then wash it in plain water containing a small amount of white vinegar, or use soap and water. Rinse well and dry with a lintless cloth. A final rubbing with a lint-free cloth often makes a window look clearer.

WOODWORK. All woodwork, regardless of the finish, needs frequent dusting. When a cleansing more thorough than dusting is needed, varnished or shellacked woodwork may be washed with a cloth wrung out of warm water containing mild soap. After rinsing and drying, furniture polish may be applied.

Apply water to waxed woodwork sparingly. If necessary, clean it by using mild soap and a little water. Wash only a small area at a time. Then rub dry. After this treatment, it is usually well to apply more wax.

HARDWOOD FINISHES AND FLOORS WAXED, OILED, OR VARNISHED. Dust the wood. Wash a small area with cloth wrung from a recommended commercial cleaner or mild soap and water.

CLOSETS. To clean the clothes closet: Remove all clothing; assort and remove the articles that are not to be put back; take out all boxes, bags, and shoes; wash and wipe dry the shelves; wipe floor, if not waxed; air the closet thoroughly; dust and replace boxes; and finally hang clothing.

Winter clothing, which is to be put away for the summer after being thoroughly brushed, or perhaps cleaned, may be placed in moth-proof cedar bags, chests, or drawers. Clothing, blankets, or rugs that are to be put away must be clean and may be wrapped to keep out the dust.

CARPET OR LARGER RUGS. If there are spots, wash spot with warm soapy water and dry thoroughly or use a good commercial cleaner. If the rug is small enough, beat it outdoors to remove dirt and dust.

DRAPERIES. Clean with a vacuum cleaner, leaving them hanging or laying them flat on a surface. If there is no vacuum cleaner, hang them out of doors and brush.

PICTURES. Clean behind the picture with a brush. Clean the frame with a soft, dry, clean cloth. Wipe glass with damp cloth and polish with dry, clean cloth.

LAMP SHADES. Brushing or cleaning with a suction cleaner are satisfactory methods for almost all shades that are not washable.

TILE AND BRICK. Clean with stiff brush and scouring powder. Do not use much water.

PAINTED SURFACES. Wash with damp cloth and mild soap. Wipe with a dry cloth.

RADIATOR. Place several layers of newspaper under radiator. Clean by using vacuum cleaner with a narrow attachment or a narrow brush.

CLEANING TOOLS

Cleaning equipment is just as important in the house as a set of good tools in a carpenter's shop or as a box of colors and brushes to the artist. Have you ever thought of cleaning as artistic work? Nothing can be beautiful unless it is clean, and you are adding to the beauty in your home, as well as to its healthfulness, in all the sweeping and dusting and washing that are so necessary.

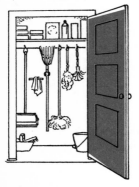

NEEDS VERSUS WANTS. To work neatly and efficiently, you need a supply of stiff brushes and soft brushes, with long handles and short handles, and plenty of cleaning cloths and paper towels.

Examination and careful study should precede all purchases made of the so-called labor-saving devices. Before buying, you will make a better purchase if you consider seriously such questions as these:

- What will this article do for me or the family?
- Why am I buying this article?
- Do I know that it is the best of its kind offered on the market?
- Will it save both time and effort?
- Is it simple to operate?
- Is it easy to take care of?
- Will I use it often enough to justify its purchase?

THE CARE OF TOOLS FOR HOUSEHOLD WORK. All the cleaning equipment should have a definite place. Every apartment and every house should have a closet built for the purpose of storing these things, and every family member should know how to care for them.

Take the proper care of the articles used in cleaning in order that they will give better service and last longer.

Brooms: Use alternate sides so that it wears evenly. After sweeping, leave it clean and ready to use again. Always hang up a broom.

Brushes: Wash in warm soapy water, rinse, and dry thoroughly. Brushes with stiff bristles may stand on bristles to dry, but those with soft bristles should stand so weight is taken off the bristles.

Mops: Wash in hot soapy water, rinse well; shake and dry thoroughly in fresh air and sunshine.

Vacuum cleaners and carpet sweepers: Empty dust container. Clean the brushes. Oil the motor according to manufacturer's directions. Always wind the cord smoothly before putting away.

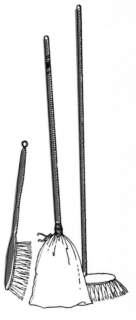

Use cold or warm water when washing brushes, as hot water will loosen the bristles if they are held in place by glue.

NATURAL CLEANSERS

Remember that sunshine and fresh air are nature's best purifiers and better than any that we can buy at a store. Natural cleaners are also safer and cheaper than the store-bought kind. They also do the job. Make sure you always have on hand: baking soda, white vinegar, and a natural scented oil. These three, combined with plain old water, can do a number of household cleaning jobs.

Table 13. Recipes for Natural Cleaners

SINK, BATHTUB, AND TOILET CLEANER	AIR FRESHENER
Baking soda alone or Baking soda and Borax mixture	Mix baking soda and lemon juice and place in small bowls around the house.
FURNITURE POLISH	DRAIN CLEANER
¼ c. vinegar Few drops olive oil Few drops lemon juice	1 c. baking soda, followed with 1 c. vinegar Plug drain, wait 30 minutes, and run hot water.
ALL-PURPOSE CLEANER #1	DISINFECTANT SPRAY
Few drops of natural soap 2 c. water Few drops lavender essential oil	1 c. hydrogen peroxide 1 c. water
ALL-PURPOSE CLEANER #2	DISINFECTANT CLEANER
½ c. baking soda or 4 tsp. Borax 1 c. vinegar 1 gal. water	½ c. Borax 1 gal. hot water
GLASS AND ALL-PURPOSE CLEANER	TILE AND GROUT CLEANER
1 c. vinegar 1 c. water	1 c. water 3 c. baking soda

ALSO, Bon-Ami, Borax, and natural castile soap are good all-around natural cleaners.

CAUTIONS IN THE HOME

The home should be a happy, cheerful place. It should also be a safe place in which to live. Safety in the home is a cooperative affair. Each member of the family should take his or her share of the responsibility for making the home a safe place for all.

Every year many people are injured by falling over things. Keep things in their proper places, where persons can learn to expect them and be prepared to protect themselves from tripping over them. People may also be injured by falling down to a lower level. Some of the chief causes of home accidents are:

- Broken window pane
- Flying curtains
- Leaning out of window
- Scissors
- Articles on floor
- Broken wire
- Electric cord lying on floor
- Vase of flowers too near edge of table
- Poisons in home
- Wood too near fire
- No fire screen
- Standing on rocker
- Frayed light cord
- Loose floor nails
- Eggs piled too high in bowl
- Iron left standing
- Pan handles pointing away from stove
- Gas oven left on
- Food boiling over
- Reading over lighted stove
- Curtains too near stove
- Articles on basement stairs
- Rugs not secure
- Poorly lighted stairways
- Slippery bathtub
- Ice-covered steps
- Flammable fluids
- Loaded firearm

Learning to slow down and to obey the rules of order is as necessary in the home as on the highway. Accidents are not as liable to occur when a home is run systematically.

ERADICATING HOUSEHOLD PESTS

Have you ever thought how many things there are that contribute to one's health and happiness? Where people live as closely together as they do in cities and towns, each person is responsible for the health and happiness of the others, and it becomes the business of each person to know and to do her part well or others will suffer through the neglect.

The homemaker's share of responsibility in this respect is large because what goes on in the home has its influence on every other home in the neighborhood. If a housekeeper pays little attention to sanitary regulations, if she does not keep her house clean and it becomes infested with cockroaches or other insects, if she is careless about the disposal of garbage or about keeping the premises tidy, the whole neighborhood suffers. Here are some of the insects that may invade your home and ways to exterminate them.

FLIES AND COCKROACHES. One of the most dangerous is the common house fly. The fly seems harmless, but once you know what places it frequents and what its habits are, you must regard it as a deadly enemy. It is usually born in filth and makes its home in manure piles, dirty spittoons, garbage cans, or decaying refuse. But it is not content to stay there; it comes straight from these repulsive places and, without even wiping its feet or asking your permission, alights on the table, takes a walk on the edge of a milk glass, crawls over icing on a cake, or feasts on sugar in a bowl.

Another pest is the cockroach. They frequent pantries, kitchens, laundries, and other places that offer food, warmth, and moisture and do their foraging when these places are deserted, usually in the dark. Roaches are so obnoxious because they, too, live in filthy places such as drain pipes and decaying animal matter. No one wants creatures of this kind running over the kitchen table, over the dishes, in the pantry, or lurking in the dish cloth or corners of the sink.

ANTS AND BEDBUGS. Yet another nuisance that housekeepers have to fight is the ant. The habits of ants are interesting to study, but their presence in the sugar bowl and other sweet foods is most annoying. They are so small that it is possible for them to get into almost any food container, even though it may seem to be well sealed. Probably the best method of getting rid of ants is to remove the food that seems to attract them, but this is difficult, for they like nearly every kind. Borax-based solutions work best.

Another pest that one should know how to control is the bedbug. Bedbugs do not live in beds only but in the cracks in walls and floors, under torn bits of wallpaper, in upholstering of furniture, and anyplace where their little flat bodies may be concealed. It is an easy matter for bedbugs to be brought into a house. An occasional bug may be brought in on the laundry or in the traveling bag after one has been stopping at a hotel. Members of families who travel a great deal should be careful to inspect their baggage and clothing before going home. To eradicate the bugs, various powders are found on the market. Washing all parts of the bedstead with boiling hot water will kill the bugs and the eggs, but of course may ruin the finish on the bed.

YOUR BEST DEFENSE. The best way to ensure oneself against all pesky invaders is to leave the kitchen, pantry, laundry, sink, garbage can, and any other place they are known to frequent *immaculately clean*, especially at night. No crumbs, no grease, no soiled dish cloth or towel should be left around. All food should be carefully covered. A generous use of borax (it has relatively low toxicity and is safe for household use) sprinkled in cracks about the sink, along baseboards, and wherever roaches or ants find runways has caused their disappearance. Traps of various kinds have been devised as well. Whatever method you choose, it must be used persistently and repeatedly.

"Play and pleasure have just as much to do with keeping us well and happy as the food we eat and the clothes we wear."

Leisurely Pursuits

As we've all heard before, "All work and no play" makes Jill a dull girl and Jack and dull boy. We have certainly come to realize that one cannot live by work alone and that time is needed for play and for life enrichment. Different people have different amounts of money, some have much more than others, but all people have the same amount of time, *24 hours* each day—no more, no less—year in and year out.

Because most of us have a limited amount of leisure, it is necessary to plan for its use to get the most fun out of it. When the homemaker wants to be sure of spending money wisely, she makes a budget, or a plan for spending and saving. A really good homemaker "budgets" her time too, and she should set apart a portion of the day for play and pleasure as well as for work. If we want to get the most out of our leisure time and do our share to help others enjoy theirs, we need to plan for it. After all, everyone likes to be free from regular work at some time during each day. Sports, gardening, needlework, entertaining, and community service are just a few of the activities we should all make time for in our busy schedules.

MAKING THE MOST OF TIME OFF

Hobbies are such fun. They are something we do in our free time because they give us much pleasure. In this way, one may find ways to express oneself in an interesting manner. Any hobby that you do in your leisure time, such as reading, writing, painting, gardening, collecting, learning to play some musical instrument, should become a real recreation from daily work. Remember to vary your hobbies so they will become more interesting.

THE BENEFITS OF PLAY AND PLEASURE.

It is just as important to plan for our pleasures as it is to plan for our meals and our clothes. Play and pleasure have just as much to do with keeping us well and happy as the food we eat and the clothes we wear. If we do not eat the right kinds of foods or wear the right kinds of clothes, our bodies will not be kept in good condition; and if we do not get enough of the right kind of pleasure, our minds and bodies suffer. Of course much of our work gives us pleasure, but no one wants to do the same thing all the time, even if it is enjoyable. The body and mind need a change.

Just as a plan for spending helps us to get the most out of our money, in exactly the same manner a plan for spending our leisure time helps us to get the most enjoyment out of that, too.

Sports: Any game, played indoors or out of doors, does its share to help pass time pleasantly and at the same time is helping you mentally and physically.

Gardening: This is an inexpensive and fascinating hobby. It is a hobby in which one can indulge quite freely. A well-planned and well-planted garden is a work of art affording pleasure to the gardener and others. (For more on this delightful avocation, see pages 158 to 161.)

Collecting: A hobby of collecting is something that every member of the family usually enjoys. Regardless of what one is collecting, whether it is stamps, pictures, coins, or books, each one can be on the lookout for interesting objects for the collection.

Reading: Not only is reading a most interesting way to spend leisure time, but its results are generally most satisfying. In the home, both magazines and books are accessible to all members of the family. Through the current home magazines, we observe what is best in design, line, and color for clothing and the home and how to make each more beautiful and attractive by the right touches.

Crafts: Any objects may be listed as crafts that require more or less artistic manual skill. This gives an opportunity to do something that one desires and in the way that one pleases, an opportunity for self-expression. Such crafts might include refinishing old furniture, weaving a rug, or knitting a scarf. If inclined toward crafts, try to have some place of your own wherein to keep the working materials and where you can work leisurely.

Volunteering: The home is no longer limited to an individual house or apartment. Actually doing something for your neighborhood creates an interest in it. Always try to make your community (whether of houses or in an apartment building) a desirable place to live. Suggest ways of making your surroundings more beautiful and attractive, as well as sanitary, and agree among yourselves to do definite things. Everyone will be the better for your community service.

THE NEEDLE ARTS

Every homemaker desires to do something a little differently. Many have been able to express this desire to create something beautiful through the needle arts of crocheting, knitting, embroidery, and cross-stitch. Crocheting is a restful and fascinating pastime for which the only tools needed are a hook and yarn. For knitting, at least two needles are needed, along with yarn and thread. If you are just starting to learn, don't succumb to discouragement. Remember: Practice makes perfect.

Let's focus here on embroidery and cross-stitch, since through these relatively simple techniques you can add just the right touch of beauty and interest to many a household article as well as a birthday or holiday gift, a dress, or napery and drapery.

EMBROIDERY. Pictures may be made not only with a brush and paint, but with needle and thread. Table 14 shows you some ways to draw by sewing.

To make beautiful stitches, follow these suggestions:
- ✓ Select the thread, floss, or yarn of a proper size, color, and texture for your design and material, and a needle of a correct size; avoid over-decoration.
- ✓ Mark the pattern clearly on the material in fine even lines.
- ✓ Do not start with a knot in your thread. Use the running stitch.
- ✓ Use an embroidery hoop to hold the cloth taut and thus avoid making the embroidery stitches too tight.
- ✓ Take special care to make stitches even in length and slanted in the same direction.
- ✓ Use no knot in embroidery but carry the thread ends in some part of the design and work over them or use tiny running stitches.
- ✓ Always press or iron embroidery on the wrong side with a bath towel underneath.

Table 14. Plain and Fancy Stitches

OUTLINE STITCH	CHAINSTITCH

Use: Outlining, stems.	Use: Outlining, filling in.
SINGLE FEATHER STITCH	SATIN STITCH

Variations: double, triple stitch.	Use: filling in; monograms.
BLANKET STITCH	FRENCH KNOT

Use: edges, filling in.	Use: center of flowers, filling in.

LAZY DAISY STITCH

Use: Petals and foliage	A quickly made stitch!

CROSS-STITCH. The cross-stitch consists of two slanting lines crossed. It is an exceedingly useful stitch that can be used to make lovely designs on bags and cushions and for initials on towels. Attractive gifts can be made for friends and neighbors or for the baby layette.

You can design your own cross-stitch using squared paper or canvas that is then basted onto your chosen material. Some materials are very coarse and can be followed without using the canvas, but on linen or other finely woven material it is necessary.

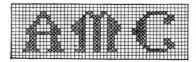

The cross-stitch is easy and very decorative.

To make the stitch, follow these directions.

1. Bring the needle up to the right side at the lower left corner of the square that the stitch would form if crossed.
2. Pass the thread slanting across the warp threads, and take the stitch on a line with the warp, pointing the needle toward you.
3. When the thread is drawn through, half the cross is made. Repeat across a whole row according to the design.
4. Finish the cross by returning from right to left with the same vertical stitches.

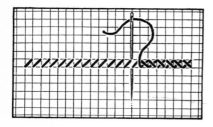

It is necessary to do the ground stitches first, then the upper stitches.

FLOWERS AND PLANTS IN THE HOME

A touch of greenery enlivens any home and brings a welcome bit of nature to your everyday life.

A FLORAL PICTURE. Every flower arrangement should be a picture. To make an artistic bouquet, the principles of design should be applied to the grouping of flowers. There should be good proportion with regard to the length of flowers and the height and width of the container. While no rules will hold in all cases, the following may serve as a guide in arranging flowers. In an *upright container*, that is, one which is taller than wide, height of flowers and foliage (above top of

the container) 1½ times height of container. In a *low container*, such as a bowl, height of flowers and foliage 1½ times average diameter or width of container. (This does not mean that all flowers and foliage should be the same height. The measurements concern the tallest flowers or foliage.)

INDOOR PLANTS. In the winter when cut flowers are not so plentiful, plants may be used instead of bouquets to decorate the home. Although most plants either require direct sunlight or grow better in it, some plants such as philodendron will grow, or at least keep alive, when not placed in direct light. Blooming house plants, whether planted in water or soil, should be grown in sunny windows. When dust accumulates, wash the foliage carefully. Plants breathe through the pores in the leaves; hence the latter should be free from dust.

TENDING A GARDEN OF DELIGHTS

Gardening can be hard work, but also extremely rewarding. Even the smallest of plots can produce not only beautiful flowers and shrubs, but nutritious vegetables and fruits for your family.

GARDEN FLOWERS. To ornament a yard, flowers should be planted to make pleasing color combinations. If you don't have a yard, a window box makes a fine miniature garden. The time of year and the duration of blooming time should also be considered. There are blossoms from the beginning to the close of the flowering season in gardens where the plants and shrubs have been carefully selected. In planting flowers in a bed or border, place the low-growing flowers around the edge or front and the taller ones in the center or rear.

For those without the space or time for a garden, a window box is a pleasing alternative.

In addition to ornamental flowering shrubs and plants, there should be flowers for cutting in a yard. When selecting flowers to plant for cutting, choose colors that will be pleasing in the rooms in which you wish to place them. Also think of the containers in which you wish to arrange the flowers.

GETTING THE GREATEST FOOD VALUE OUT OF YOUR GARDEN. In various ways the soil can be made to yield two crops where only one has been grown before. For example, two crops can be planted simultaneously in the same space, the one to mature quickly and the other slowly. Radishes or other fast-growing plants can be sown with parsnips, carrots, melons, and other plants of slow growth. The radishes will break the ground and thus help their slow-growing comrades to push up through the soil, and they will be matured and eaten before the slower plants need the space.

Fast-growing plants like lettuce can be interplanted between cabbage plants, both in the rows and between the rows. Where hand cultivation is practiced, it is usually possible to grow plants closer together than is commonly done. Cabbages, ordinarily set two feet apart, can be planted at intervals of 18 inches, potato rows two feet apart, and so on.

The gardener will find that, if she fertilizes the soil properly, plants will grow all the better for being so close together, for they will shade the ground effectively and thus assist greatly in conserving the water in the soil. As soon as one crop is harvested, another should take its place. For instance, early potatoes can be followed by turnips, peas by celery, early beans by late cabbage, and so on.

There is also no reason why a householder with a moderate-size yard should not have a succession of both fruits and vegetables. Anyone, by taking thought, can plan and enjoy a succession of bush and tree fruits of either the dwarf or standard sizes, according to the space at her command.

If we organize our gardening so as to produce maximum food value, and do our gardening in the same spirit we have shown in doing other work, we shall be amazed at the results.

Gardening and other outdoor work helps to keep the body well.

SAVING AND PRESERVING SEED. This is the most important branch of the gardener's business. Only the truest plants should be selected; that is to say, such as one of the most perfect shape and quality. In the cabbage, seek small stem, well-formed loaf, few spare or loose leaves; in the turnip, large bulk, small neck, slender stalked leaves, solid flesh or pulp; in the radish, high color (if red or scarlet), small neck, few and short leaves and long top. The marks of perfection of each plant are well known, and none but perfect plants should be saved for seed.

Table 15. How Long to Save Your Seeds

TYPE	YEARS	TYPE	YEARS
Asparagus	4	Corn	3
Bean	1	Cress	2
Bean (Kidney)	1	Cucumber	10
Beet	10	Dandelion	10
Burnet	6	Dock	1
Cabbage	4	Fennel	5
Camomile	2	Garlic	3
Capsicum	2	Gourd	10
Caraway	4	Hop	2
Carrot	1	Horse Radish	4
Cauliflower	4	Hyssop	6
Celery	10	Jerusalem Artichoke	3
Marigold	3	Lavender	2
Melon	10	Leek	2
Mint	4	Lettuce	3
Mustard	4	Mangle Wurzel	10
Onion	2	Rutabaga	4
Parsley	6	Savory	2
Parsnip	1	Sorrel	7
Peas	1	Spinach	4
Pennyroyal	2	Squash	10
Potato	3	Tansey	3
Pumpkin	10	Thyme	2
Radish	2	Tomato	2
Rhubarb	1	Turnip	4
Rosemary	3	Wormwood	2

The seed pods should stand till perfectly ripe, if possible. They should be cut, pulled, or gathered when it is dry; and they should, if possible, be dry as dry can be before they are threshed out. If, when threshed, any moisture remains about them, they should be placed in the sun, or near a fire in a dry room, and when quite dry should be put into bags and hung up against a very dry wall where they will by no accident get damp. The best place is some room or place where there is occasionally at least a fire kept in winter.

Thus preserved, kept from open air and from damp, the seeds of vegetables will keep sound and good for sowing for the number of years stated in Table 15. Some of the seeds in this list will keep sometimes a year longer if very well saved and very well preserved, especially if closely kept from exposure to the open air. But to lose a crop from unsoundness of seed is a sad thing, and it is indeed negligence wholly inexcusable to sow seed the soundness of which you are not certain.

KEEPING CHICKENS. Even the smallest urban plots may provide enough room to raise chickens. When properly managed, chickens are a source of considerable profit, yielding more for the food they consume than any other stock. All grain is food for them, including millet, rice, sunflower, flax, and hemp. They are also fond of milk, and indeed scarcely any edible escapes their notice, including garden pests. They carefully pick up most of the waste garbage around the premises. A hen house may be constructed in various ways, and when tastefully built it is an ornament to the premises. If properly taken care of, chickens will more than earn their keep.

THE ART OF ENTERTAINING

To make a guest comfortable and happy is the constant endeavor of the thoughtful hostess. Whether guests are to spend the afternoon, stay for a meal, or remain overnight, she is mindful of their physical comfort. She directs them definitely when, how, and where to come; she has the house at proper temperature. If food is served to the guests, she shows a hospitable spirit by having it as tasty as possible. However, if something goes wrong in preparing or serving the food, her apologies are not so profuse and long drawn out that the guests are bored.

FOR THE OVERNIGHT GUESTS. A thoughtful hostess sees to it that there is a comfortable bed, inviting with its clean sheets and other coverings; drawer and closet storage for clothes, the latter equipped with plenty of hangers; a frequently replenished supply of bath and face towels and washcloths, hung on a certain rack if the guest uses the family bathroom; a water glass; a soap dish with a fresh bar of soap; writing materials, in case the guest wants to write letters or cards; a lamp near the bed; a waste-paper basket; a magazine or two, suitable for bedtime or vacation reading.

A good hostess makes sure her guest has an inviting, comfortable bed.

But just as important as care for a guest's physical welfare is the sociable attitude of the hostess and other members of the family. A guest should be made to feel welcome and that his or her presence is a pleasure to the entire household.

PLANNING A PARTY. A certain amount of entertaining is necessary, even if one goes to the extent of believing with Byron that society is only a polished horde, "Formed of two mighty tribes, the bores and the bored." To the hostess who does not try to entertain beyond her means or her strength, the bringing together of friends should be a pleasure. Too frequently the pleasure is greater on the part of guest than of hostess.

Entertainment of large groups is easily achieved by carrying out a set program. When planning a party, it is perhaps most important to invite congenial guests. It is not so necessary that all guests be acquainted as it is to have persons with similar ideas or interests. Often one or two new friends add interest to a group.

After the guests are decided upon come the invitations. A verbal invitation, usually by way of the telephone, an informal note, or formal engraved card, is the usual type of party invitation. If a telephone invitation is given, the reply is, of course, made while at the phone. If an informal note is sent, the same form of note should be sent in reply. A similar procedure should be followed if a formal invitation is received. A reply to an invitation should be of the same type as the invitation. It should also be definite, that is, there should be no question.

Keep in mind such suggestions as these:
- Plan the number of guests; invite guests who will be congenial.
- Plan the amount of help available.
- Plan the amount of time needed for preparation.
- Plan a form of entertainment that will interest all.
- Plan the menu; the kind and amount of food needed.
- Plan the preparation of dishes, silver, and linen to be used.
- Plan the cost, including the expense of everything.

A clever homemaker can arrange tasks that visitors can comfortably perform and that relieve her from too many details.

FRIENDLY VISITS. Entertaining real friends in our homes, and in turn visiting them in theirs, brings much pleasure. When a friend comes to call, it is a graceful gesture of hospitality to serve a cup of tea or other beverage and perhaps a sandwich, wafer, or cake. Such an occasion is known as an *informal tea*. A cup of tea warms the heart, stimulates conversation, and provides an atmosphere of good fellowship. For an informal tea, the hour is anytime between three and six o'clock in the afternoon.

At an informal tea, tea is served in the living room, sun room, or on the porch or lawn, not in the dining room. If either a large tray or a tea wagon is used, the beverage, food, and dishes may be easily carried into the room where the guests are seated. The tray should be placed on a conveniently high table, beside which the hostess may sit to pour.

On the tray or tea wagon are needed: teapot filled with hot tea; cream and bowl of sugar, sugar spoon; cups, dessert plates (or saucers), teaspoons, napkins; plate of breads, such as sandwiches, cinnamon toast, toasted scones, tiny hot biscuits or muffins; plate of small cakes or cookies; dish of orange marmalade or other preserve, spoon for serving; and punch bowl and glasses.

CHILDREN'S PARTIES. If you give a party for very young children, you should expect to entertain not only the children but the mothers or some older persons who will accompany the children. Children's parties usually require a good deal of supervision. It is usually advisable to invite children of about the same age as the child for whom the party is given, and they should not be kept too long. Unless there are several persons to help you, do not invite too many guests. Three or four children, assembled under conditions that suggest a party, usually have a happy time.

Entertainments: A hunt of some kind, whether it be for apples, eggs, or miscellaneous trinkets, invariably delights children who are at least five years old. Entertainment of this kind usually serves to acquaint children with each other. A hunt is a good first game if several other games are planned. Blowing up balloons and making bubbles never fail to delight children. Also, children like not only to sing but to act out the words of well-loved songs. Be ready with a couple tunes.

Refreshments: Paper hats, as well as other favors placed at each cover of a party table, always delight children and carry over the entertainment into refreshment time. Mothers who make it a rule that the children of their households eat no sweets between meals are sometimes disturbed when sweets are served at a party midway between luncheon and dinner. To avoid such a situation, it is sensible to substitute for afternoon sweets a simple dinner and plain cake or cocoa.

Stories: It is a mistake to frighten little children with harrowing stories involving cruelty. Ghost stories should never be told to children, for they have not learned to recognize the difference between the truth and make-believe. Everything is real to them. There are many illustrated books containing wholesome stories for children. A visit to the public library will enable you to get these books or others suggested by the librarian.

HOSTESSING A BUFFET

Informal meals served buffet style are very popular for several reasons. First, more guests can be served comfortably than would be possible in a small home, if they were seated at a dining table. And second, the informality makes it enjoyable to most guests.

ARRANGEMENT OF FOOD AND DISHES FOR BUFFET SERVING. The two most striking differences between the buffet style of serving and other styles are that each person helps himself to food from general serving dishes, and that no one sits at the dining table to eat. For this style of serving, the dining table, dishes, and food may be arranged as below. Usually all food, with the possible exception of the dessert, is placed on the table in general serving dishes before the meal is announced. A serving spoon or fork or both is placed beside each dish.

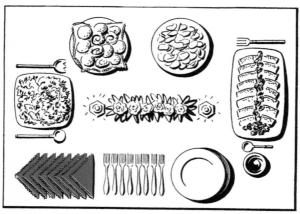

A buffet supper table may include salad, rolls, side dish of vegetables, and a main dish. *Dishes and Decorations:* Napkins, plates in pile, forks, flowers and candles. *Not shown:* Ice cream and cake.

METHOD OF SERVING. Some hostesses provide a tray for each guest. Each tray may be covered with a mat or napkin or may be left uncovered, depending upon its material or finish. On each tray, a napkin, fork, and spoon may be placed. Or the trays may be piled together so that each guest can take one, cafeteria style, and then collect his or her own napkin, fork, and spoon.

Tray or not, each guest takes a plate and begins to place food on it, helping himself from the various dishes spread out on the buffet table. Often the hostess has asked one or two friends to sit at the table and serve the main dish or beverage, or each person may wait on himself. When the plates are filled, each guest seats himself anywhere he chooses. A thoughtful hostess often places small tables near chairs in the living room, where her guests may sit and eat in comfort.

Second helpings may be passed to the guests, or the guests may go to the buffet table. The dessert may be served either way. After eating, each guest may take his tray or dessert plate to the buffet table, or the host or hostess may carry the soiled plates to the kitchen. A wheel tray is a convenience at this time.

FOODS SUITABLE FOR BUFFET SERVICE. Any informal meal—breakfast, luncheon, or supper—may be served buffet. However, not all foods served at breakfast, luncheon, or supper are suitable for buffet serving. Foods easily eaten with a fork or spoon are best for buffet service. Breads or rolls may be buttered before they are placed on the buffet table, so that knives will not be needed. Foods that cannot be kept warm after cooking or baking and that require immediate service are unsuitable for a buffet meal. Exceptions to this rule are such foods as waffles, which are browned at the buffet table, or foods cooked in a chafing dish or on a grill. Hot foods can be served from a casserole or chafing dish, or a covered double-compartment serving dish.

PICNICS AND OUTDOOR FUN

Plans for a picnic are so often met with whoops of joy from every member of a group. A picnic means getting away from the meals at home. There is so much fun and good companionship at a meal served in a woody glen or near the banks of a lake or stream.

LAYING A PICNIC FIRE. The fuel for outdoor cooking may be dried leaves and sticks found in the woods, or charcoal carried from home. The stove may be built by assembling the stones of the fields, or it may be a metal grid brought with the picnic supplies.

If a fire is built in the woods, a place should be selected where there can be no danger of forest fires. Lay the fuel materials carefully so that they will burn briskly. When the blaze of burning fuel disappears, leaving glowing coals, the foods may be cooked. Some foods that are tasty and suitable for out-of-door cooking are:

Broiled frankfurters: Place frankfurters in a wire broiler, or use sticks 18 inches or more in length, first peeling the bark from them and pointing one end. Hold the frankfurters over glowing coals and cook until browned. Insert each in a picnic roll that has been split and buttered at home. Serve hot.

Hamburger patties: Prepare patties at home. Wrap each patty in waxed paper. At the picnic, heat an iron or aluminum skillet over the glowing coals. When it is hot, grease with a piece of bacon. Cook the patties until brown.

Grilled corn: Soak unhusked corn in water 30 minutes. Remove from the water; drain. Place on a grill over glowing embers. Cook the corn for about 30 minutes or until done. (Test by removing an ear and pulling back the husk.) In serving, pull back the husks and eat the corn with butter and salt.

Kabobs: Small pieces of beef, bacon, with vegetables or fruits strung on a pointed stick and broiled, are known as kabobs. Here are some suggestions for tasty combinations of foods cooked on a stick.

1. Frankfurters cut in half-inch slices and each slice wrapped in bacon.
2. Cubes of tender uncooked beef alternating with pieces of onion (preferably Bermuda) or with halves of small unpeeled tomatoes.
3. Very small sausages alternating with half-inch apple slices.

OUTDOOR VACATIONS. A vacation does not always mean not to work at all, but just changing one's occupation. Planning and spending a holiday or vacation is one of the best ways to get the most fun out of leisure time. What is more fun than a camping trip? Even working on a garden would be an interesting way to spend part of the day. Spending time in nature is one of life's most rewarding and relaxing pursuits. Vacations need not be expensive. You should decide on what you can afford and try to take some kind of vacation once a year.

If for some reason or other a fire is not to be built at a picnic, much of the food to be served can be prepared at home, including sandwiches, meat loaf, baked ham, and casseroles.

INDEX

CREDITS

Home Economics: Vintage Advice and Practical Science for the 21st-Century Household features text excerpts and illustrations from the following sources, all of which are in the public domain:

Child's Health, Book Three, by John A. Thackston and James F. Thackston (The Economy Co., 1936).
Developing Our Health, Grade Six, by John A. Thackston and James F. Thackston (The Economy Co., 1947).
Domestic Science: Principles and Application, by Pearl L. Bailey (Webb Publishing Co., 1921).
The Farmer's New Guide for Farm, Field, and Fireside, by H. H. McClure, Thomas Bond, and Frederick H. Osgood (John E. Potter and Co., 1893).
Elementary Home Economics, by Mary Lockwood Matthews (Little, Brown, and Co., 1921).
"Furnishing the Small Apartment," by Clara L. Ernst, in *The Ladies Home Journal* (November 1919).
Girl Scout Handbook: Intermediate Program (Girl Scouts of the United States of America, 1947).
"Getting the Greatest Food Value Out of Your Garden," by Lewis Edwin Theiss, in *The Ladies Home Journal* (March 1919).
Health and Safety (The Continental Press, Inc., n.d.).
Health and Safety First Steps, Gale Smith (Hayes School Publishing Co., Inc., Benton Review Publishing Co., Inc., 1946).
The Home and the Family: An Elementary Textbook of Home Making, by Helen Kinne and Anna M. Cooley (The Macmillan Co., 1917).
Homemaking for Teen-Agers, Book One, by Irene E. McDermott and Florence W. Nicholas (Chas A. Bennett Co., 1951).
Homemaking for Teen-Agers, Book Two, by Irene E. McDermott and Florence W. Nicholas, Chas A. Bennett Co., Inc., 1958).
Household Arts for Home and School: Volume I, by Anna M. Cooley and Wilhelmina H. Spohr, The Macmillan Co., 1920).
Household Arts for Home and School: Volume II, by Anna M. Cooley and Wilhelmina H. Spohr, The Macmillan Co., 1920).
Household Science and Arts, by Josephine Morris (American Book Co., 1912).
Infant Care, Children's Bureau Publication no. 8 (U.S. Government Printing Office, 1938).
Junior Food and Clothing, by Kate Kinyon and L. Thomas Hopkins; illustrations by Dorothy Rittenhouse Morgan (Benj. H. Sanborn & Co., 1928).
Meat: Selection, Preparation, and 100 Ways to Serve (Armour and Company, 1932).
Modern Physiology, Hygiene, and Health: The Play House, by Mary S. Haviland; illustrations by Margaret F. Browne (J. B. Lippincott Company, 1921).
The Mode in Dress and Home, by Dulcie Godlove Donovan; illustrations by Eulalie (Allyn and Bacon, 1935).
Physics of the Home: A Textbook for Students of Home Economics, by Frederick A. Osborn (McGraw-Hill Book Co., 1929).
Practical Home Economics, by Alice M. Donnelly and Helen Cramp (D. E. Cunningham & Co., 1919).

The Science and Art of Homemaking, by Mary W. Cauley (American Book Co., 1935).

Shelter and Clothing, by Helen Kinne and Anna M. Cooley (The Macmillan Company, 1913).

Sportsmanlike Driving (American Automobile Association, 1947).

Woman's Institute Library of Dressmaking: Care of Clothing, by The Woman's Institute of Domestic Arts and Sciences (International Educational Publishing Co., 1925).

Young Folks at Home: Home Economics for Junior High School, by Florence LaGanke Harris and Treva E. Kauffman; illustrations by Beatrice Magnuson Derwinski (D. C. Heath and Co., 1948).

Your Home and You, by Carlotta C. Greer (Allyn and Bacon, 1948).

Illustrations

METRIC CONVERSIONS

SYMBOL	WHEN YOU KNOW	MULTIPLY BY	TO FIND	SYMBOL
Mass				
oz.	ounces	28	grams	g.
lb	pounds	.45	kilograms	kg.
Volume				
tsp.	teaspoon	5	milliliters	ml
tbs.	tablespoon	15	milliliters	ml
fl oz.	fluid ounces	30	milliliters	ml
c.	cups	.24	liters	l
pt.	pints	.47	liters	l
qt.	quarts	.95	liters	l
gal.	gallons	3.8	liters	l
Length				
in	inches	2.5	centimeters	cm
ft.	feet	30	centimeters	cm
yd.	yards	.9	meters	m
Temperature				
°F	Fahrenheit	.555 after subtracting 32	Celsius	°C

Spoonfuls

¼ tsp.	1.25 milliliters
½ tsp.	2.5 milliliters
1 tsp.	5 milliliters
¼ tbs.	3.75 milliliters
½ tbs.	7.5 milliliters
1 tbs.	15 milliliters

Fluid Ounces

¼ oz.	7.5 milliliters
½ oz.	15 milliliters
1 oz.	30 milliliters

Cups

¼ cup	59 milliliters
½ cup	118 milliliters
1 cup	236 milliliters

Pints, Quarts, Gallons

½ pint	236 milliliters
1 pint	473 milliliters
1 quart	946.3 milliliters
1 gallon	3785 milliliters

Weight in Ounces

¼ oz.	7.1 grams
½ oz.	14.17 grams
¾ oz.	21.27 grams
1 oz.	28.35 grams

Pounds

¼ lb.	.113 kilograms
½ lb.	.227 kilograms
¾ lb.	.340 kilograms
1 lb.	.454 kilograms

Length

1 inch	2.544 centimeters
1 foot	30.48 centimeters
1 yard	91.44 centimeters

Temperature

212° F	100° Celsius
325° F	163 °C
350° F	177° C
400° F	204° C
425° F	218° C

TO THE READERS OF THIS BOOK

This book gives only a taste of all the interesting things you will wish to learn about the home economics and the homemaking studies. For more helpful, practical, and economical advice, visit VintageHomeEc.com.
Are you not eager to know more?